THE MESSENGER OF ALLAH
A BIOGRAPHY OF MUHAMMAD RASULULLAH
(Salla Allahu Alaihi Wa Sallam)

SENIOR LEVEL — PART I

IQRA' PROGRAM OF SÎRAH

Part of

*A Comprehensive and Systematic Program of
Islamic Studies*

Abidullah al-Ansari Ghazi
Ph.D. Harvard

Tasneema Khatoon Ghazi
Ph.D. Minnesota

**IQRA' INTERNATIONAL EDUCATIONAL FOUNDATION
Chicago**

Part of a Comprehensive and Systematic Program of Islamic Studies

A Textbook for the Program of Sirah Senior Level

The Messenger of Allah Textbook: Part One

Chief Program Editors
Dr. Abidullah al-Ansari Ghazi
Ph.D., Harvard University

Tasneema Khatoon Ghazi
Ph.D., University of Minnesota

Religious Review
Rabita al-Alam al-Islami
Makkah Mukarramah

Copyright © 1991, IQRA' International Educational Foundation. All Rights Reserved.

Printed March, 2011
Printed in India by Gopsons Papers Ltd

Special note on copyright:
This book is a part of IQRA's comprehensive and systematic program of Islamic Education.

No part of this book may be reproduced by any means including photocopying, electronic, mechanical, recording, or otherwise without the written consent of the publisher. In specific cases, permission is granted on written request to publish or translate IQRA's works. For information regarding permission, write to:
IQRA' International Educational Foundation,
7450 Skokie Blvd., Skokie, IL 60077
Tel: 847-673-4072; Fax: 847-673-4095
E-mail: iqra@aol.com
Website: http://www.iqra.org

Library of Congress Control Number: Pending
ISBN # 1-56316-160-5

INTERNATIONAL AWARD

CERTIFICATE OF DISTINCTION
Awarded by
The Government of Islamic Republic of Pakistan

to the authors for writing:
Six textbooks of Sirah
Our Prophet I, II
Mercy to Mankind I, II
Messenger of Allah, I, II

12 Rabi' 1404
18 December 1983

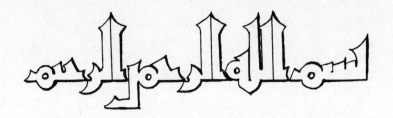

Dedicated to *Sahabah* (R)

Ridwan Allah Alaihim Ajma'in
(May Allah be pleased with them all)

And to those who followed the *Sahabah* (R)
in their good deeds.

وَالسَّابِقُونَ الْأَوَّلُونَ مِنَ الْمُهَاجِرِينَ وَالْأَنْصَارِ وَالَّذِينَ اتَّبَعُوهُمْ بِإِحْسَانٍ رَضِيَ اللَّهُ عَنْهُمْ وَرَضُوا عَنْهُ وَأَعَدَّ لَهُمْ جَنَّاتٍ تَجْرِي تَحْتَهَا الْأَنْهَارُ خَالِدِينَ فِيهَا أَبَدًا ۚ ذَٰلِكَ الْفَوْزُ الْعَظِيمُ ﴿١٠٠﴾
التوبة ٩

And the first, who led the way to Islam,
the *Muhajirun* and the *Ansar*,

And those who followed them in their good deeds,

Allah is pleased with them
and they are well pleased with Him.

And Allah has made ready for them *Jannah*
underneath which rivers flow.

There they will live for ever.

This is the greatest success.

al-Tawbah 9:100

CONTENTS

	Introduction	I
	Map	II
Lesson 1	*Jahiliyya:* The Days of Ignorance	1
Lesson 2	Birth and Early Childhood	5
Lesson 3	Muhammad's Early Years	10
Lesson 4	Early Career and Marriage	14
Lesson 5	The First *Wahi* (Revelation)	17
Lesson 6	First Muslims	20
Lesson 7	General Invitation to Islam	24
Lesson 8	The Miracle of the Quran	28
Lesson 9	Persecution and First *Hijrah*	32
Lesson 10	Hamzah and Umar Accept Islam	35
Lesson 11	*Kuffar's* Offer Rejected; Muslims' Social Boycott Begins	38
Lesson 12	Opposition of the *Kuffar*	41
Lesson 13	Failure in Taif	44
Lesson 14	*Isra'* and *Mi'raj:* Journey to al-Quds (Jerusalem) and Ascension to Heaven	48
Lesson 15	Success in Yathrib (Madinah)	51
Lesson 16	Why Didn't the *Kuffar* Believe in Rasulullah(S)?	55
Lesson 17	Why Did Muslims Believe in Rasulullah(S)?	61
Lesson 18	*Hijrah* of Rasulullah	65
Lesson 19	*Kuffar* Search for Rasulullah (S)	68

INTRODUCTION
THE PROGRAM OF SIRAH
For Teachers and Parents

All praises are due to Allah, *Subhanahu wa Ta'ala*, who has guided us and enabled us to complete these textbooks on the *Sirah* of Rasulullah, *Salla Allahu alaihi wa Salam*. May Allah also give us strength to complete this project of Islamic education for our children and make these books beneficial for every child (*Amin*).

These two textbooks are part of a comprehensive and integrated program of Islamic education in general and the *Sirah* of Rasulullah (S) in particular. *Sirah* textbooks are prepared at three levels, viz:

Elementary	ages	6—8
Junior	ages	9—11
Senior	ages	12 and over

These textbooks and workbooks should be used for teaching Sirah in school and at home.

The authors recommend the use of workbooks, and other enrichment literature with the text. **They are available now.** The program of Islamic Studies has been developed to fill the existing gaps in the field of Islamic Studies for our children and youth. It incorporates modern educational ideas and techniques to facilitate the task of learning.

Certain specific characteristics of these *Textbooks* are:

1. These books have been written with a controlled vocabulary. This will make the reading of the text easier for the children at their respective levels.

2. In spite of the fact that the vocabulary is controlled, Islamic vocabulary is introduced to enable our children to learn Islamic terminology and use it in every day life.

3. New and difficult words are repeated especially at elementary levels to provide sufficient opportunity for learning.

4. New words, both English and Arabic, are given at the end of each lesson. The teacher should provide extra practice in teaching them.

5. Each lesson is summed up under three important points. This provides an opportunity to focus on the main ideas and to help comprehension. Further comprehension drills shall be provided in Skill-Books and other educational aid material.

6. These textbooks contain basic information about the life of *Rasulullah* (S) that a child should know. The stories are separated from the biographical information.

7. The Sirah stories and other educational aid material are being prepared by the writers separately. **The Sirah stories are now available in eleven parts.**

8. The text integrates the basic message of the Quran and other aspects of Islamic education with *Sirah*. This Islamic curricular integration gradually develops through two levels, elementary and junior, and is finally presented in a comprehensive way at the Senior level.

9. At the elementary level, we have discussed the Makkah period in greater detail; at the Junior level, this order is reversed. This scheme was warranted keeping in mind the conceptual development of the young children and the events of the life of *Rasulullah* (S) in Makkah and in Madinah. At Senior level both periods receive equal attention and interpretation of various aspects of *Sirah* is provided.

10. *The Messenger of Allah*, **Senior level, integrates the** *Sirah* **with Quranic Studies by offering relevant readings from the Quran in the text and giving a Quranic Study question for further study of the Quran. Thus through these textbooks a student will grasp the central message of the Quran and see its chronological development and relationship to the** *Sirah*. **The** *Quranic Study* **questions will provide the student a systematic introduction to the study of the Quran. The teachers are advised to study each question themselves before assigning it to the class.**
The workbooks include the exercises on the Quranic Studies.

11. The contents of the books have received careful religious reviews from Islamic scholars. The books have also been edited professionally.

12. We have made an effort to have these books beautifully illustrated. We have not, unfortunately, achieved satisfactory success in this. We hope future editions will make up for this deficiency.

13. This educational endeavor is unique and comprehensive. It has taken painstaking labor, careful research, serious efforts of four years by the authors and help from many individuals and sources to produce these textbooks in the present form, but their full potential will only be realized once the whole program is produced and implemented. It will be another two or three years before everything is complete, *Insha Allah*.

14. These books, we hope, shall provide the model for similar work on other aspects of Islamic Studies and, hopefully, shall be a starting point for a systematic, scientific and continuous effort by all concerned individuals and organizations, in this direction.

15. A detailed Teachers/Parents Guide for the individual textbooks will be prepared after the completion of the *Sirah* Project, *Insha Allah*.

16. These books are the beginning of the fulfillment of our long aspirations and we pray to Allah to give us strength and bless our lives to bring this effort to conclusion. As far as we are concerned we have *al-Hamdu li Allah*, made a life-long commitment to Islamic educational work and request your *Dua* and support.

17. The establishment of *Iqra' International Education Foundation*, by concerned Muslims in Chicago (USA) aims to promote Islamic education. We hope this work will now proceed faster and more systemically. We need the support, cooperation and prayers of every concertned Muslim to promote the cause of Islamic education.

Abidullah al-Ansari Ghazi
Tasneema Khatoon Ghazi

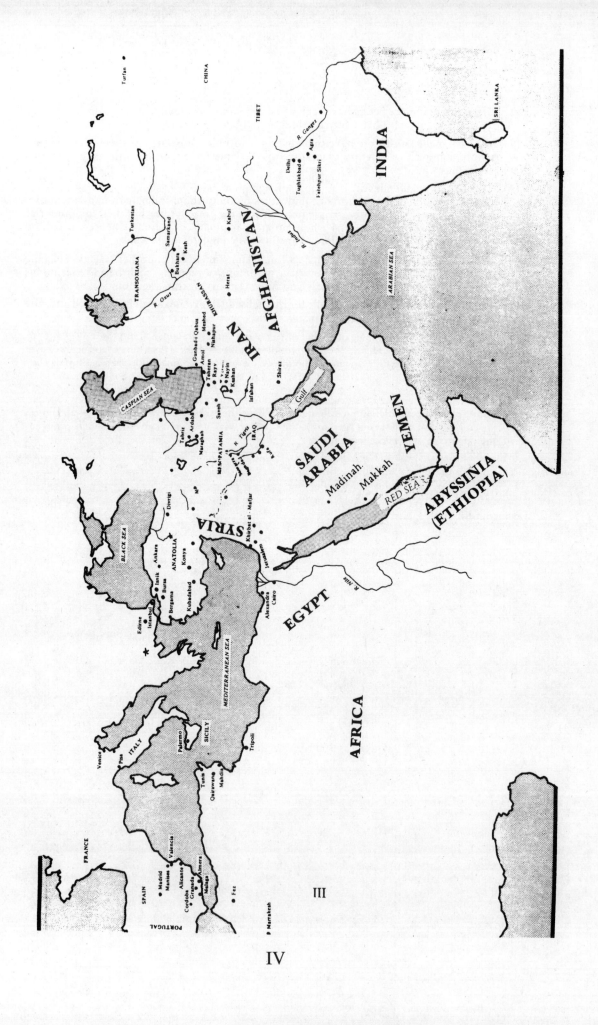

LESSON 1

JAHILIYYAH: THE DAYS OF IGNORANCE

It was a Monday morning of 12 *Rabi I* (20 April 571)[1], nearly fourteen hundred years ago, Rasulullah, *Salla Allahu alaihi wa Sallam*[2] (may Peace and Blessings be upon him), was born in Makkah. Makkah was, and still is, a very important city of Arabia. It was regarded as a holy city by all the Arabs. In it was situated Kabah, the main house of worship for all the Arabs.

Kabah was built by Prophet Ibrahim, *Alaihi al Salam*[3] (peace be upon him), and Prophet Ismail, *Alaihi al Salam* (peace be upon him), for the worship of Allah. These two prophets, like all the other prophets, preached the religion of Islam. They are regarded by the Arabs as their ancestors. Most Arabs are their children; others became their children by believing in their teachings. For many years after the death of Ibrahim (A) and Ismail (A), Kabah remained a place of pilgrimage for all Muslims. They came to Kabah from all around Arabia to worship Allah.

Slowly the descendants of Ibrahim (A) and Ismail (A) forgot about the pure religion of Islam. They started *Kufr*. *Kufr* is being ungrateful to Allah, and worshipping idols and images in place of Allah. Some of them believed that their gods and goddesses shared Allah's power. This kind of belief is called *Shirk*. It is the greatest sin in the eyes of Allah.

Kabah remained a center of worship, the holy temple for all the Arabs. It housed their three hundred and sixty-five idols. Arabs gathered in Makkah each year for pilgrimage. Some of them even walked around Kabah naked. There was a big fair where they gambled and got drunk and consulted sorcerers and magicians for their future plans.

Few Arabs still remembered the teachings of Islam and worshipped only Allah. They were called *hanif*. Other Arabs who did not like their idol-worshipping religion became Christians or Jews.

[1] According to some accounts Rasulullah(S) was born on 9 *Rabi I*.

[2] Allah says in the Quran, "Indeed Allah and His angels send their blessings upon the Prophet, O believers, ask Allah's blessings upon him and salute him with worthy salutation." *al-Ahzab* 33:56. In our book an (S) after the name of Rasulullah is an abreviation of *Salla Allahu alaihi wa Sallam* to remind us to send salutations.

[3] We ask for Allah's blessings for the prophets and angels by these words. An (A) after the name of a prophet or an angel reminds readers to ask Allah's blessings upon him.

Makkah was an independent city. It was ruled by the tribe of Quraish. Banu Hashim, the family of Hashim (Hashim was a famous Quraish chief), was caretaker of Kabah. Service to pilgrims and care of Kabah was a great honor. Quraish were respected all over Arabia because of their services to the pilgrims and responsibility for the care and maintenance of Kabah.

The land around Makkah was mostly barren. There was no agriculture. Most of the Quraish were business people. They sent two caravans for trade each year. In winter their caravan went to the South and in summer it went to the North. Though robbing caravans was a normal way of life in Arabia, the caravan of the Quraish was respected by all and no one dared to rob it. The custody of Kabah made them rich; it gave them both national respect and a life of peace.

The Quraish, instead of being thankful to Allah, became an insolent people. They believed they were superior to others. They oppressed the poor, the slaves, the orphans, and the widows. They cheated in business. They buried their daughters alive and mistreated their women. Women had no rights in Arab society. A man could take as many wives as he wished and divorce them at will. Women had no right to inherit property.

Arabs were divided into clans and tribes. Clans and smaller tribes were allied with bigger tribes. Only a few tribes lived in the city but most of them wandered in search of pasture and water. Arabia was mostly a vast desert and had only a few oases. The bedouin Arabs loved to wander in the desert. They were very proud of their freedom.

Each tribe was ruled by a chief called the *Shaikh*. He was generally the oldest member of the tribe. The Arabs were fond of their language. Poets were especially respected for their poetic compositions. Good speakers and story tellers were held in honor. It was a matter of great distinction to speak the pure Arabic language. The desert tribes spoke beautiful Arabic. The Makkan Arabs sent their children to live with the desert Arabs to learn their language.

Arabs had forgotten not only *Tawhid*, the belief in one God, but also most of the good things that Ibrahim (A) and Ismail (A) had taught them. The tribes fought against each other all the time. They believed in retaliation and revenge. They would never forgive or forget. So the tribal wars continued for years and years. The tribes would kill their enemies, plunder their properties, and take possession of their children and women.

Arabs also had some good qualities. They were a brave people. They were very generous. They treated their guests kindly. They usually kept their promises. They were frank and told what they believed. They were ready to fight for their beliefs. However, without right beliefs and high moral standards these good characteristics alone could not make the Arabs a great people.

The religious situation in the rest of the world was not much different from the one in Arabia. Allah had sent His prophets and guides to all nations to guide people to the path of true faith of Islam. The prophets taught about *Tawhid* (Allah's Oneness) and moral life. Like the Arabs, people in the world who had received Allah's revelation were far away from the pure religion of Islam They changed the teachings of their prophets. The *kufr* and the *shirk* were common among them. In their evil ways they were like the Arabs.

In the world there were many nations and tribes. People of each race believed that they were superior to other people. The strong nations fought and suppressed the weaker nations.

The Arab world was surrounded by two powerful empires. In the East was the Iranian Empire ruled by the Khusraws. Their religion was Zoroastrianism. The Zoroastrians worshipped fire and believed in the dualism of good and evil spirits. That means that the power of good and evil are equally strong and are struggling against each other.

In the West was the Eastern Roman or Byzantian Empire ruled by the Caesars Their religion was Christianity. The Christians believed in the doctrine of the Trinity. The Trinity means that God consists of three persons; God the Father, Isa (Jesus) the Son, and the Holy Spirit. Thus, the Christians believed in the divine nature of Prophet Isa (Jesus), whom they accepted as the only begotten Son of God.

The Iranian and Byzantian empires had constant wars between them. The Arabs lands lay in between the two empires. Each of the two empires controlled many Arab lands. The Arabs had no strong state of their own. They were politically weak and socially divided.

The world was waiting for someone to come: to remove the evils of the world; to teach mankind *Tawhid*, the worship of One and only One God, Allah; and to unite the warring nations into one brotherhood, the *Ummah* (community) of Islam.

Long before the birth of Rasulullah (S), Allah's many revelations to mankind spoke about his coming. Every prophet in his lifetime had received from Allah the good news of Rasulullah's coming. Many prophets, knowing that the Muslim *Ummah* is dear to Allah, even desired to be born in the *ummah* of Muhammad (S). The time had come when Allah would send His last prophet to teach mankind His perfect religion, Islam, and give His final revelation, the Quran, to His prophet.

Points of review:

1. The descendants of Ibrahim (A) forgot the pure religion of Islam and started *Kufr* and *Shirk*.
2. The Quraish tribe ruled in Makkah. They regarded themselves superior to others.
3. Other religious communities also corrupted the pure revelations. The world was waiting for Allah's final revelation.

Words to remember:

Custody, dualism, *Hanif*, insolent, *Kufr*, retaliation, *Shirk*, *Tawhid*, Zoroastrianism.

Quranic study

Early Makkan *Surahs* speak about the conditions of Arabian society. Study the following *Surahs*:

1. *al-Fajr* 89:17-20; *al-'Alaq* 96:6-13; *al-Takathur* 102; *al-Ma'un* 107

See what characteristics of the Arabs they criticise.

2. The Quran says the religion of Ibrahim was not Judaism, Christianity, or paganism but Islam. Read the following:

i. *al-Baqarah* 2:130-135; ii. *Ali Imran* 3:67; iii.*al-Nahl* 16:120-123

LESSON 2

BIRTH AND EARLY CHILDHOOD

Rasulullah (S) belonged to the tribe of Quraish and family of Banu Hashim. His father's name was Abdullah. His mother's name was Aminah. Abdullah and Aminah had a very happy life.

Aminah became pregnant. Most women are happy when they get pregnant, but Aminah had more reason to be happy. She had a dream. In the dream, someone told her, "You will have a son. He will be the leader of mankind. You should name him Muhammad." She was delighted. While she was pregnant she felt happy and healthy all the time.

Aminah's husband, Abdullah, died suddenly while visiting Yathrib. Aminah was sad and concerned about her unborn son. "Who will raise him? Who will teach him? Who will care for him?" She asked herself. Aminah's father-in-law, Abd al-Muttalib, was very old. Abdullah's brother was Abu Talib, who had a large family and was, himself, poor. The future of her child made Aminah sad and worried. Although such ideas came to Aminah's mind, she was told in her dreams about the great blessing that her son would be. These good tidings gave her strength and pleased her.

Many other signs were noted which told of a great event to come. One such famous event was the failure of a big attack on Makkah by the powerful Abyssinian ruler, Abraha. He came with a mighty army of elephants to destroy Kabah. The Makkans were weak and helpless. They left the care of Kabah in the hands of Allah. Allah sent small birds carrying little stones in their claws. The birds pelted Abraha's army with the little stones, killing his elephants and making his army flee. Many people felt that if Allah had saved his Kabah from destruction he must have some plan for it in the future.

When Muhammad (S) was born, fourteen towers of the palace of the Khusraw of Iran fell down. The great fire which had been burning for one thousand years in the Zoroastrian temple of Iran was extinguished. Through these signs Allah foretold that His prophet would bring the power of mighty rulers down; that Allah's worship would replace the worship of fire and other such objects.

The Sacred Mosque (Niebuhr)

Two views of *Masjid-al-Haram* in Makkah

Among the Makkan Arabs, it was a custom to give their children to foster parents who came from desert villages. These mothers took the children with them and kept them in the clean and open climate of the village. The villagers also spoke good Arabic. Makkans wanted their children to learn to speak well. When they grew up they might become great poets, story tellers, and speakers.

At that time, many women from the tribe of Banu Sa'd came to take children from the Makkan families. They went to the rich families and got all the children of the Quraish. Nobody wanted Muhammad (S), the orphan child of Abdullah.

There was a poor lady, Halimah, who was late to arrive. Her camel was thin and slow. Her donkey was weak and exhausted. She herself was so weak that she did not have enough milk even for her own infant son.

She could find no other child to take with her so she went to Aminah and Abd al-Muttalib for baby Muhammad (S). Aminah gladly gave her son, Muhammad (S), to Halimah. Halimah did not know that this baby was chosen by Allah to be a blessing for all mankind. Soon he would fill Halimah's own life with blessings.

As Halimah and her husband departed for home, she saw the blessings all around her. Her camel gave lots of milk, enough for her whole family. Her camel and her donkey now ran so fast that all the others were left behind. Other women of Banu Sa'd called to her, "Halimah, wait for us," but her donkey would not stop. Halimah herself now had lots of milk, enough for her son and for baby Muhammad (S).

Halimah's village had been suffering from drought for a long time. There was no pasture for the goats and camels. There were no crops for the people. As soon as baby Muhammad (S) came to the village, it rained, and the drought was soon over. All the goats and camels became healthy. The villagers had a good crop.

The whole village came to know that the new baby had brought them luck and blessings. All of them loved Muhammad (S). His foster mother, Halimah, loved him like her own children. She knew Muhammad (S) was not an ordinary baby. Halimah and her husband would have liked to keep Muhammad (S) with them permanently, but when Muhammad (S) was two years old they took him back to his mother, Aminah, and his grandfather, Abd al-Muttalib.

Halimah wanted to keep Muhammad (S) for a longer time. She convinced Aminah and Abd al-Muttalib to let her keep baby Muhammad (S) for some more time. Aminah wanted the baby to be returned to her but because of her concern for baby Muhammad's health she allowed Halimah to take him with her.

Muhammad (S) played with his foster brothers and sisters. He went with them to the desert to shepherd their goats. One day, Muhammad (S) and his foster brothers saw two men in white clothes coming toward them. These were, in fact, angels of Allah. They went straight to Muhammad (S), opened his chest, took his heart out, cleaned it, filled it with Nur, the divine light, and put it back.

All the children were scared. They ran home and told their parents. The parents rushed back to Muhammad (S) to see if he was all right. They saw baby Muhammad (S) sitting there. He was also a little frightened. He was still looking up to the heavens watching the angels depart. He told them about his experience.

Muhammad's foster parents did not know what all this meant. They took Muhammad (S) to an astrologer. When the astrologer looked at Muhammad (S) he knew that Muhammad (S) was going to be a great man. He also saw that he would break the idols and abolish idol worship. He started screaming, "Kill Muhammad now before he grows up and brings our religion down."

This screaming scared the foster parents. They went home worried about Muhammad's safety. Halimah was so scared by these incidents that she took Muhammad(S) back to his mother and grandfather. Muhammad(S) had lived for about four years with his foster parents and foster brothers and sisters.

When Prophet Muhammad (S) grew old he always remembered his foster parents kindly. His foster family remembered his childhood fondly. Halimah's family always talked about the blessings and pleasures which baby Muhammad (S) had brought to them. Later, when Prophet Muhammad (S) started preaching Islam, all of his foster family became Muslims. They had seen the blessings of the baby Muhammad(S). They were ready to receive the blessings of Muhammad, Rasulullah (S).

Rasulullah (S) always remembered Halimah with love and called her with affection, "my mother."

Points of review:
1. Before the birth of Muhammad (S), many signs foretold a big event.
2. Muhammad (S) lived with the family of Halimah in Banu Sa d for four years.
3. The family of Halimah and the village of Banu Sa'd experienced many blessings with the coming of Muhammad (S)

Words to remember:
Astrologer, extinguish, *Nur*, pelt.

Important names
Abd al-Muttalib, Abdullah, Abu Talib, Aminah, Banu Hashim, Banu Sa'd, Halimah.

Quranic Study:

1. The Quraish, being the custodians of *(Bait Allah)* Ka'bah, enjoyed respect, peace and security in Arabia. Read *Surah Quraish*, 106 and see how Allah wanted the Quraish to respond to the favors of Allah.

2. Read the story of Isma'il's sacrifice, *al-Saffat*, 37:99-111. Ibrahim (A) and the building of Ka'bah, *al-Baqarah*, 2:124-128; *Ali Imran* 3:96-97.

3. Prophet Ibrahim (A) prayed to Allah for the birth of Muhammad (S). *al-Baqarah* 2:129 and Allah heard the prayers of Ibrahim and sent Muhammad (S) as His last prophet, *(al-Baqarah* 2:151).

How do these two verses describe the mission of Rasulullah?

LESSON 3

MUHAMMAD'S EARLY YEARS

Muhammad (S) now lived with his mother and grandfather. His grandfather, Abd al-Muttalib loved him and showed him great affection. Muhammad (S) reminded him of his dead son, Abdullah.

After some time, Muhammad's mother, Aminah took him to the city of Yathrib to meet some relatives and to visit her husband's grave. The city of Yathrib is now known as Madinah. Aminah died on her way back to Makkah. Muhammad (S) was very sad. He was brought back to Makkah by a maid servant.

His grandfather, Abd al-Muttalib took charge of him. Abd al-Muttalib would not leave Muhammad (S) alone even for a short while. Muhammad (S) became greatly attached to him. He became like both father and mother to him. Two years later, Abd al-Muttalib also died.

This left Muhammad (S) sad and lonely once again. Muhammad (S) suffered a lot as a child. It was, perhaps, Allah's way of teaching Muhammad (S) kindness and concern for the orphans, the poor, and the helpless. Allah showed us through the example of Prophet Muhammad's sufferings that Allah's protection is always with the orphans and the helpless.

Muhammad's uncle, Abu Talib, now became his guardian. Abu Talib cared for him just as he was his own child. Muhammad (S) was not like any other child. The Makkan youths wasted their time in fairs and indecent games, but Muhammad(S) worked as a shepherd and gave his earnings to his uncle. The Makkan youths did not mind being naked before others; Muhammad(S) was modest and bashful. Muhammad(S) was different from them in every respect. The evils of the Makkan life did not touch him. He was kind, polite and respectful. Everyone loved him and praised him.

Muhammad (S) always spoke the truth. As he grew to be a young man, people were impressed by his truthfulness. They called him *al-Sadiq*, the truthful one. They also trusted Muhammad (S). People called him *al-Amin*, the trustworthy one. His truthfulness and trustworthiness became so famous that when someone said *al-Sadiq*, the truthful one, or *al-Amin*, the trustwortrhy one, people would know that he was talking about Muhammad (S).

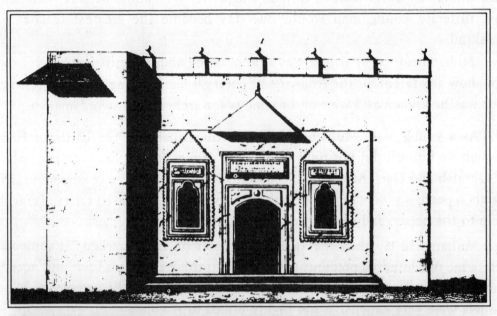

The Well of Zamzam (Aly Bey)

At that time very few people in Makkah knew how to read or write. Muhammad's uncle, who was poor, could not send him to a teacher, so Muhammad (S) never learned to read and write. Who could believe then that this illiterate young man would one day become the greatest teacher of mankind.

Muhammad (S) by nature was a peaceloving and reflective person. He did not show any talent for the Arab arts of poetry, speech giving and story telling. Nor was he known as a warrior, or famous for archery and swordsmanship.

As a young man, Muhammad (S) saw the tribal war, the battle of Fijar, though he himself did not fight in the war. It was fought between the tribes of Quraish and Qais. After much bloodshed, at the initiative of some Quraish chiefs, a peace was concluded. It established peace and promised safety of travel, help to the needy, and support for the oppressed.

Muhammad (S) liked the agreement. Later on he remarked, "If someone offers me one hundred precious red camels for this agreement I will not accept them. I am still ready to help anyone under the terms of the agreement." Red camels were very expensive and highly prized in Arabia.

Muhammad (S) grew up a handsome, healthy young man, respected by everyone. He spoke politely, respected his elders, showed love to children, and helped widows, orphans, and the poor. He did not waste his time in useless games. He did not go to parties. Like other Arabs, he never drank or gambled or walked naked around Kabah. He never worshipped idols. Though Muhammad (S) was an orphan, Allah protected him from the evil ways of the young men of Makkah.

After Muhammad (S) became Rasulullah, Allah reminded him of the hardships of his childhood and youth and promised a better future for him:

> For you the future will be better than the past life.
> In the future your Lord will give you so much, you will be well pleased.
> Did Allah not find you an orphan and gave you shelter?
> Did Allah not find you searching for truth and guide you?
> Did Allah not find you poor and make you rich?
> Therefore, do not oppress the orphan.
> Therefore, do not drive away the beggar.
> But proclaim the bounties of your Lord.
>
> *al-Duha* 94:4-11

Points of review:
1. Muhammad (S) lost his mother and grandfather at a young age. His uncle, Abu Talib, raised him.
2. Muhammad (S) was known as *al-Sadiq* and *al-Amin*.
3. Muhammad (S) liked and valued the peace agreement.

Words to remember:
al-Amin, al-Sadiq, reflective, talent.

Important names:
The Battle of Fijar

Quranic Study:
1. Read *Surah al-Inshirah* 94. It was revealed soon after *Surah al-Duha* and deals with the same theme.

LESSON 4

EARLY CAREER AND MARRIAGE

Muhammad's uncle, Abu Talib, like most other Quraish, was a businessman. He took Muhammad (S) with him on business trips. Abu Talib did not want to leave Muhammad (S) alone. Also, he wanted to teach him the rules of trade.

As a boy of eleven, on one of his trips to Syria, Muhammad (S) met a Christian monk Buhaira. Buhaira told Abu Talib that Muhammad(S) would have a great future and that he must specially safeguard him.

When Muhammad (S) grew up, he started his own business. He had no money of his own. He was well known for his honesty. People wanted him to use their money for business and share in the profit.

At that time there was a rich widow living in Makkah. Her name was Khadijah. Because of her good nature, she was called *Tahirah*, "the pure one". She asked Muhammad (S) to do business on her behalf. Muhammad (S) agreed and took a caravan of merchandise for Khadijah.

Khadijah sent her slave, Maisarah, with him. During the travels, Muhammad (S) treated the slave very kindly. Maisarah also saw how honest Muhammad (S) was. Maisarah noticed many good qualities in Muhammad (S) which no other Makkan possessed. He also saw that a cloud protected Muhammad (S) from the heat of the summer sun.

A Christian monk named Nastur met Muhammad(S) and Maisarah in Syria. He was very impressed by Muhammad (S). He told Maisarah that Muhammad (S) had all the signs of prophethood. Maisarah also saw many other miracles of Muhammad (S). More than miracles, he was impressed by Muhammad's beautiful manners and charming personality. He discovered that Muhammad (S) was both fair and honest in his business dealings.

Muhammad (S) returned to Makkah after this successful business trip with a big profit from Khadijah's merchandise. On his return, Maisarah told Khadijah what he had observed. He told her how Muhammad (S) was different from other people whom Maisarah had met during his travels or had seen in Makkah. Khadijah was so impressed by Muhammad (S) that she proposed marriage to him.

She was forty years old and a widow with three children. Muhammad (S) was twenty-five and still unmarried. Muhammad (S) accepted the proposal. He wanted a wife who was honest, had good manners, and was kind. They remained married for twenty-five years until the death of Khadijah separated them. They loved and respected each other. It was an ideal marriage. The Prophet (S) had six children with her. She had the honor of being the first person to accept Islam. She was a great support for Muhammad (S) in his mission as Allah's prophet.

The marriage with Khadijah made Muhammad (S) a wealthy man but he was not interested in wealth. He wanted to help the poor and the needy. Khadijah presented Muhammad (S) with a slave, Zaid. Muhammad (S) freed Zaid immediately and asked him to go back to his parents. Zaid's parents came to take him with them but Zaid was so attached to his kind master that he never left. He was one of the first Muslims and became a close *Sahabi* (Companion) of the Prophet (S).

Khadijah was a very generous woman. She loved Muhammad (S) and was ready to do everything for him. Both Muhammad (S) and Khadijah gave much of their wealth away and freed their slaves.

Points of review:
1. Muhammad (S) learned business from his uncle, Abu Talib, and became a successful businessman.
2. At the age of twenty-five, Muhammad (S) married Khadijah. They had six children.
3. Muhammad (S) and Khadijah gave away much of their wealth and freed their slaves.

Words to remember:
Monk, *Sahabi*, *Tahira*.

Important names
Buhaira, Khadijah, Maisarah, Zaid.

Quaranic Study:
1. Islam permits trade, encourages charity, and prohibits usury. Read *al-Baqara* 2:275-76
2. The Quran encourages a special kind of trade. Read *al-Saff* 61:10-13 and see what that trade is.

1. The Kabah   2. Old city of Makkah   3. Cave of Hira (Bio-visual, Hyderabad)

LESSON 5

THE FIRST WAHI (REVELATION)

Slowly Muhammad (S) lost his interest in the business. He felt sad to see the Arabs fighting and killing each other. He did not like to see them worship idols and follow the evil ways. He did not know what he could do. He was neither a scholar nor a philosopher. He was neither a poet nor a speaker. In fact, he was not even educated. He wondered what he could do to help the Makkans.

He became more and more withdrawn from the world. He would go to a cave called Hira and pray to Allah quietly. He would take with him food and water to last for several days. His wife, Khadijah, would also bring him more food and water if he did not return home after several days. Khadijah wanted to help Muhammad (S) in every possible way to find the Truth. Muhammad (S) was forty years old, and his heart was restless in search of Truth.

Once, in the month of Ramadan, Muhammad (S) was praying in the cave of Hira when the Angel Jibril (A) (Gabriel) appeared to him. He was not expecting to see anyone in that lonely cave, much less an angel. He was, naturally, frightened to see Jibril (A). Jibril (A) greeted him and told him, "Read!".

As Muhammad (S) did not know how to read he replied, "I cannot read."

The angel squeezed his arm and embraced him tightly and commanded him again, "Read." Muhammad (S) again replied, "I do not know how to read." Angel Jibril, once again, for the third time, squeezed Muhammad's arm and embraced him tightly. Muhammad (S) felt exhausted but his heart was now ready to receive *Wahi*, the divine revelation. The Angel recited the first verses of the first *Wahi* and Muhammad (S) repeated after him,

> Recite, in the name of your Lord,
> who has created mankind from
> a clot of blood.
> Recite and your Lord is generous.
> He taught man to write with pen,
> and He taught man what he did not know.
> *al-Alaq* 96:1-5

This was the first *Wahi*, the beginning of the revelation of the Quran from Allah to His last Prophet (S). This was the start of Muhammad's mission as Rasulullah, a Prophet and Messenger of Allah. Gradually, in the next twenty-three years, Allah completed the revelation of His last book, the Quran, to His prophet, to teach mankind His perfect religion, Islam.

Jibril (A) taught Muhammad (S) how to make *Wadu* (ablution) and say *Salat* (prayer). Then Jibril (A) left.

Receiving *Wahi* through an angel was a strange experience for Muhammad (S). He was fearful and nervous and immediately left for home. He had always shared everything with Khadijah. He wanted to tell all this to her. She might know what had happened to him and what could be done about it. As he reached home, he was shivering and was feeling cold. He asked his wife to place a blanket upon him. Then he told her of his strange experience.

She did not understand the nature of her husband's experience, but she knew of her husband's great qualities. So she felt confident that Allah would safeguard him from every evil force. She comforted him saying, "Allah will always protect you. You are kind to your relatives, you help the poor and support the weak, you comfort the orphans and the widows, you are hospitable to your guests, and you love truth. Allah does not harm such people. Allah saves and guides such people."

The next morning, she took Muhammad (S) to her old cousin, Waraqa Ibn Nawfal, a learned Christian who had studied the Bible. Waraqa knew that in the Bible Allah promised to send a new messenger who would comfort mankind and teach them good morals. Waraqa told Muhammad (S) and Khadijah, "I think it is the same angel Namus who earlier visited Musa (A) and other prophets as well. It seems that Allah has chosen Muhammad(S) to be His prophet. His people will persecute him and expel him for his teachings."

Who the prophets were and what they did, Muhammad (S) did not know exactly. Waraqa's words comforted Muhammad (S), but he did not have any knowledge of Bible. Muhammad (S) did not know how to read to find out about the mission of the prophets. He wondered what Allah wanted him to do for His cause. He asked Waraqa, "Why would my people persecute me for this? Waraqa replied, "No prophet can remain unopposed. Whenever a prophet brings the message of truth to the people they oppose him and show their hostility."

Muhammad (S) had to wait for some time. Allah, through Jibril (A), would teach His prophet about the work of the past prophets and about his own future mission for mankind. Allah would give to Muhammad (S) the knowledge of Islam, His final and perfect religion. No human being had ever had it or would have it so perfectly.

Points of review:

1. In the month of Ramadan, Angel Jibril(A) brought the first *Wahi* to Prophet Muhammad (S).
2. Prophet Muhammad (S) was scared; his wife, Khadijah, comforted him.
3. Waraqa Ibn Nawfal told Muhammad (S) that Allah had perhaps chosen him as His prophet.

Words to remember:

Clot of blood, hospitable, hostility, *Salat*, scholar, *Wadu*, philosopher, *Wahi*.

Important names

Jibril, Namus, Waraqa Ibn Nawfal.

LESSON 6

FIRST MUSLIMS

Early Years of Prophethood

Muhammad (S), son of Abdullah, the orphaned and illiterate boy of Makkah, was now Muhammad, Rasulullah, Allah's messenger and prophet, and a teacher for mankind.

For those who believed in him, he was no longer Muhammad but Rasulullah, through whom Allah had guided them to His chosen faith of Islam. For some time, Rasulullah (S) was scared and worried. The experience of Hira and its effects were still fresh in his mind. Then he developed a desire to receive more *Wahi*. During those days, Rasulullah (S) kept himself covered with blankets because of his worries. Then came the second *Wahi* telling him,

> O' you, wrapped in the blankets,
> stand up and warn.
> Magnify your Lord,
> clean your clothes
> and keep from all unclean practices.
> *al-Mudaththir* 74:1-5

The time of waiting for Rasulullah (S) was in fact a time for his preparation to receive the Quran. No human soul could bear the burden of the divine message. It needed special cleaning — purification and preparation — for a human heart to be ready to receive Allah's word. It is not even easy for mountains to bear this burden. Allah says in the Quran,

> If we had sent down this Quran on a mountain, You, O Muhammad, would indeed have seen it humbled and cracked with the fear of Allah.
> *al-Hashr* 59:21

Rasulullah (S) was now ready to receive further revelations and stand up for the cause of Allah. He was given a clear message. He was the last prophet and messenger of Allah and must teach about *Tawhid*, (Allah's Oneness) and invite all to the right path of Islam. Angel Jibril visited him more frequently and taught him what he had not known before. He received the divine knowledge, which no other human being possessed.

Rasulullah (S) first informed his family and closest friends that he was Rasulullah. He invited them to Islam. They knew him well. His wife, Khadijah, was the first woman; Ali, his cousin, was the first youth; Abu Bakr, his friend, was the first man; and Zaid, his freed slave, was the first slave to accept Islam. All of them accepted Islam because they knew Rasulullah (S) very well. They believed in him and knew whatever he spoke was always the truth.

People who became Muslims during the Prophet's life-time and saw him are called *Sahabah*, the companions (one companion is called *Sahabi*). *Sahabah* saw Rasulullah (S) and received their Islam directly from Rasulullah (S). They struggled with him for the cause of Islam. Allah was pleased with them. They are honored by all the Muslims. When Muslims hear any one of them being mentioned, they say, "*Radi Allahu Ta'ala 'anhu,*" (May Allah be pleased with him).[3]

A few more people accepted Islam through the efforts of Rasulullah and his *Sahabah*. The names of some of the prominent *Sahabah* of this period are: Uthman Ghani(R), Zubair(R), Abd al-Rahman(R), Sa'd bin Abi Waqqas(R), and Talha(R). All these were early Muslims and played an important role in the history of Islam. In the first three years, Rasulullah(S) trained his *Sahabah* spiritually for the great future task of Islam. The future would tell us how perfect this training was and how these people benefitted from their close relation to Rasulullah(S).

Points of review:
1. After a waiting period, Rasulullah (S) received the second *Wahi*, which asked him to stand up for the cause of Allah.
2. Some of his family and close friends accepted Islam.
3. These *Sahabah* received Rasulullah's training and played an important role in the history of Islam.

Words to remember:
Sahabi, Sahabiyah, Tawhid

---

[3]Blessings for a *sahabiyah* (woman companion) is "*Radi Allahu Taala anaha*" (May Allah be pleased with her.) For Sahabah in general is "*Radi Allahu Taala anhum*" (May Allah be pleased with them). An (R) after the names of the prophet's companions is a reminder to invoke Allah's blessings for them.

Important names
Abd al-Rahman(R), Abu Bakr(R), Ali(R), Sa'ad bin Abi Waqqas(R), Talha(R), Uthman(R), Zaid(R), Zubair(R).

Quranic Study
Read *Surah Muzammil* 73: 1-10 and *Surah Mudaththir* 74: 1-7. Allah is asking his prophet to prepare himself for his prophetic mission. What are those requirements? Can these also help an Islamic worker in his mission?

Lo! (the mountains) As-Safā and Al-Marwah are among the indications of Allah.

إِنَّ الصَّفَا وَالْمَرْوَةَ مِنْ شَعَآئِرِ اللهِ

The hillock al-Safa, Mecca (Aly Bey)

The hillock al-Marwa, Mecca (Aly Bey)

A Nineteenth Century view of Safa and Marwah

LESSON 7

GENERAL INVITATION TO ISLAM

Third Year of Prophethood

Rasulullah (S) had been receiving *Wahi* continuously. It told him that Islam was chosen by Allah as the last religion for all mankind. He was Allah's last prophet and he was asked by Allah, "So proclaim that (Islam) which you are commanded to proclaim, and keep away from idolators." *(al-Hijr* 15:94).

One day, Rasulullah (S) invited everyone in Makkah to come to the hill of Safa. He wanted to tell them of a great danger which the Makkans faced because of their *Kufr* and *Shirk.* The hill of Safa is close to Kabah. Rasulullah (S) stood up on the hill of Safa and asked the people, "What do you think of me ?"

Everyone responded "You are *al-Sadiq* (the truthful one) and *al-Amin* (trustworthy one)."

Then Rasulullah (S) asked, "Would you believe me if I tell you that there is an army behind this mountain which is ready to attack you?"

"Yes, of course, we will. You have always spoken the truth. You have always held our trust." The people answered.

"Then listen!" Rasulullah (S) said. "I warn you of even greater danger. There will be a Day of Judgment. You will be judged for your beliefs and actions. I invite you to believe in Allah. Give up your idols. Give up your evil practices. And do good deeds."

These people did not like these ideas. They loved their idols. The rich Quraish were used to their evil ways and did not believe that anybody has a right to judge them. They were angry with Rasulullah (S).

One of Muhammad's uncles, Abu Lahab, who did not believe in Islam said, "Is that what you wanted to tell us ? You have wasted our time."

Though people respected Rasulullah (S) for his truth and honesty, it did not help him. Some people thought he was insane to talk of such unheard-of things. No one was willing to accept his call. Now people started spreading all kinds of false rumours about him.

On another day Rasulullah (S) invited all his relatives for a dinner. After dinner Rasulullah stood up and addressed his guests in these words, "O members of my family, and chiefs of the Quraish. Today I am going to speak to you about something that no Arab youth has ever spoken. If you will follow it you will receive the well-being of this world and the hereafter."

His guests were very pleased to hear his remarks. They asked him eagerly, "What is it, O Muhammad, that could benefit us in this world as well as in the hereafter?"

Rasulullah (S) said, "Say with me, *La ilaha illa Allah* (There is no god but Allah). You will benefit in both worlds."

His cousin, Ali, who was thirteen years old was the only one who stood up and promised to help Rasulullah (S). Other relatives became annoyed and left him.

One day, Rasulullah (S) went to Kabah and openly invited people to accept the teaching of Islam. The *Kuffar* had gathered there to worship their idols. They were enraged by his remarks and attacked him. His life was saved but one of his *Sahabi*, Harith bin Hala (R), was killed by the *Kuffar*.

As Rasulullah (S) began to preach openly, more and more Makkans opposed him and became his enemies. Some *Kuffar* became the worst enemies of Rasulullah (S) and the Muslims. The *Kuffar* were rich and powerful. Their wealth and power made them proud and obstinate.

In the beginning, there were only a few converts; most of them were weak and poor. Rasulullah (S) and his *Sahabah* (R) had a very difficult task ahead of them.

Point of review:

1. Allah asked Rasulullah (S) to invite all the Makkans to accept Islam.
2. Rasulullah (S) invited the Makkans to the hill of Safa and spoke to them about the dangers of the hereafter.
3. He started inviting the Makkans to Islam publicly, but most people became angry at him and hostile to him.

Words to remember:

Kuffar, respond, task.

Important names
Abu Lahab, Harith bin Hala (R), Safa.

Quranic Study

Read *Surah al-Lail* 92. It describes two kinds of people: Those faithful to Allah and the proud independent ones. What are the characteristics of each group?

This, in fact, was the division of Muslims and *Kuffar* in Makkah.

LESSON 8

THE MIRACLE OF THE QURAN

As Rasulullah (S) invited everyone to accept Islam, the *Kuffar* began opposing him more vigorously. The *Kuffar* opposed Islam in various ways. In the beginning, an effective way was to spread lies and slander against Rasulullah (S). The message of Islam was simple and Rasulullah (S) did not show any miracles on demand. But Allah had given him the miracle of Quran.

The Arabs were very proud of their language. Poets and speakers were held in high honor. The Quran, in the perfection of its language and the purity of its message, was unique and had no equal. Any Arab who listened to the Quran knew that it was so perfect that no human being could have written it. In fact, no one could copy its style. Besides, people knew very well that Muhammad (S) had very little education and could not write such a powerful message.

Allah in the Quran challenged the *Kuffar*: "Say O Muhammad, if men and jinns unite to produce a Quran like this, they will not succeed in producing the one like this, though they may help each other." (al-Isra'. 17:88). Allah has challenged the *Kuffar* in many other places; no one ever dared to accept this challenge.

The personality and piety of Rasulullah (S) also made a deep impression upon people. Anyone who met him immediately recognized that Muhammad (S) was not an ordinary person. Many people who met Muhammad (S) and listened to the Quran became Muslims.

The *Kuffar* thought that the best way to stop the progress of Islam was to stop the people from meeting Muhammad (S). They decided to spread all kinds of rumours about him: "He has gone crazy, he is a magician, he is possessed by jinns, he is a poet, etc." They went around convincing the people not to go to Muhammad (S). Allah consoled Rasulullah (S) and criticised the *Kuffar*:

> You are not, thanks to the favor of
> your Lord, a madman.
> Indeed, you will receive a lasting reward.
> Indeed, you possess a magnificent nature.
> You will see and they will see
> which of you is mad.
>
> *al-Qalam 68:2-6*

Most people, hearing the propaganda of the *Kuffar* were afraid to meet Rasulullah (S) and listen to the Quran. Only a few wanted to know the truth for themselves and risked meeting him.

Such a seeker of truth was Abu Dharr Ghiffari, who belonged to the tribe of Ghiffar. He heard about Rasulullah (S) and the message of Islam. He also leanrned that Rasulullah's own people had become his enemies. Abu Dharr decided to travel to Makkah to see Rasulullah (S) himself. He was afraid of the Makkans' anger so he met Rasulullah (S) secretly. He listened attentively to the Quran. He was so impressed by the message of the Quran and the personality of Rasulullah(S) that he immediately became a Muslim.

His heart was now full of love for Allah and His prophet. Acceptance of the truth made him bold. Abu Dharr was not afraid of the *Kuffar* anymore. He felt so bold that he went to Kabah and announced *Shahadah*, "La ilaha illa Allah Muhammadun Rasulullah, (There is no god but Allah and Muhammad is HIs messenger.)" The *Kuffar* were enraged that a foreigner had accepted Islam and insulted their gods. Abu Dharr was beatern by *Kuffar*. He kept on repeating, "There is no god but Allah." He was saved by some Makkans who knew him and feared the reprisal of the brave tribe of the Ghiffar. Abu Dharr (R) became one of the closest and dearest companions of Rasulullah(S). He spent all his life with Rasulullah(S). Through Abu Dharr's efforts most of his own tribesmen became Muslims in the early stages of the Makkan period.

There was another person, a great Arab poet named Tufail, from the tribe of Dus. He was visiting Makkah and heard the strange rumours about Rasulullah (S). He believed in his gods, so he trusted the Makkans for whatever they said about Rasulullah (S). Whenever he saw Rasulullah (S) reading the Quran, he tried not to hear it. When he went to Kabah he kept his ears stuffed with cotton for fear of learning the Quran by mistake.

One morning he went to Kabah. He saw Rasulullal (S) saying prayers. He was reciting the Quran in his beautiful voice. Tufail said to himself, "I am a famous poet. All people think I am a very wise person. They come to me for consultation and advice. Why should I be scared of Muhammad? I should hear the Quran and decide for myself."

He cleared the cotton from his ears. He heard the beautiful recitation of the Quran by Rasulullah (S). His heart trembled when he heard Allah's message.

Tufail was deeply moved. He wanted to know more about Islam but he was afraid of the Makkans, so he quietly followed Rasulullah (S) to his house.

He asked Rasulullah (S) to recite the Quran, and Rasulullah (S) recited some verses. They are so beautiful, so simple, so clear. No human being could have written them. Tufail became a Muslim immediately. He no longer cared what people would tell him or how they would treat him. Tufail(R) is remembered as a *Sahabi* of Rasulullah (S).

The propaganda of the *Kuffar*, perhaps slowed down the progress of Islam. But Islam's progress could not be stopped. There were always some people who wanted to know the truth. Once they heard the Quran their hearts opened to the truth of Islam. They recognized that the Quran is indeed a miracle and divine revelation, and Muhammad (S) is Allah's messenger.

Points to review:

1. To stop people from meeting Rasulullah (S), the *Kuffar* spread all kinds of rumors.
2. Some people like Abu Dharr (R) and Tufail (R) met Rasulullah (S), inspite of the rumors.
3. They heard the Quran and became Muslims

Words to remember:

Propaganda, reprisal, *Shahadah*.

Important names

Abu Dharr Ghiffari, Tufail Dusi

Quranic Study

1. Read *Surah al-Qalam* 68:1-15. See how Allah challenges the *Kuffar* and criticises them for opposing the Prophet.
2. Read *Surahs: al-Isra'* 17:88-89; *al-Tur* 52:34; *al-Baqarah* 2:23-24

See how Allah has challenged the *Kuffar* to produce the likeness of the Quran.

Thanks to the efforts and sufferings of these early Muslims, Islam is the most dominant religion of the African Continent.

A modern East African Mosque, built in 1956 at Wandegeya, Kampala, Uganda, by the African Muslims of Uganda.

The world famous wood and clay Great Mosque of Djenne, built sometime during the fourteenth century, in what is present-day Mali.

(From *Islam Insurgent* by *Prof. T.B. Irving*)

LESSON 9

PERSECUTION AND FIRST HIJRAH

Most of the early converts to Islam were slaves, orphans, and widows, who were badly treated by the Makkans. They accepted Islam because Islam taught fairness and equality for all. These poor people didn't have influence or power, so by accepting Islam they exposed themselves to the anger of their masters. They belonged to an underprivileged class, and by becoming Muslims they suffered even more at the hands of the *Kuffar*. Their conversion was not only a challenge to the pagan faith, but also a revolt against an unjust social order.

To stop the Muslims from worshipping Allah, the *Kuffar*, under the leadership of Abu Jahl and Rasulullah's uncle, Abu Lahab, tortured them in every possible way. Sometimes they put the Muslims on burning sand and placed hot stones on their chests. They would punish the Muslims by dipping them in hot water. They placed ropes around their necks and dragged them in the streets. The Muslims were stoned and beaten mercilessly. The names of Bilal (R), Yassir (R), his wife Sumayyah(R) and son Ammar(R), Khabbab(R), Suhaib(R) and Abu Fukaiha (R), will always be remembered with great love by Muslims because of their sufferings.

Rasulullah (S) himself suffered all kinds of insults. Thorns were placed in his way. Garbage, dirt, and smelly camels' intestines were thrown at him. People laughed and mocked him. Rasulullah (S) and the Muslims remained patient and prayed to Allah for help.

As the opposition of the *Kuffar* to Islam increased, Rasulullah(S) advised some of the Muslims to migrate and seek refuge in the Christian kingdom of Abyssinia (also called Ethiopia). The Christians believed in Allah. They were the "People of the Book" *(Ahl al-Kitab)*. That means they received divine revelation and gospels, and they were the *Ummah* of prophet Isa(A). By sending Makkan Muslims to a Christian Kingdom Rasulullah(S) showed that relationship in Islam is not based on ties of family, race or language but on ties of common faith and common hopes. Rasulullah(S) hoped the Christian king would protect the Muslims. On Rasulullah's advice a party of eleven men and five women migrated to Abyssinia.

The *Kuffar* had business ties in Abyssinia and carried some influence in the court. They followed the Muslims there also. They wanted to catch the Muslims to punish them for their escape. They requested King Najashi to hand over the Muslims to them.

King Najashi (Negus) of Abyssinia was a pious Christian. He was not influenced by the plea of the *Kuffar* and decided to talk to the Muslims about their Prophet (S) and their religion. The Muslims chose Jafar (R) to represent them before the king. He went to the royal court and explained to the king:

> We walked in the darkness of evil and did not know the right path. We worshipped idols of stone and led unclean lives. We had no respect for human beings, neighbors, or guests. We used to kill and steal. Allah has been kind to us and sent his prophet. We know him very well, he is kind, truthful, trustworthy, and pious. He invited us to Islam. He taught us *Tawhid*, the worship of Allah alone. He teaches us to speak the truth and to keep our trust, to respect the rights of our women and orphans, our poor and our neighbors. We believed in Muhammad as a Prophet. We are Muslims. Because of the acceptance of the truth of Islam our own people have become our enemies. They persecuted us in Makkah and now they have followed us here. They want to kill us because of our faith.

The king was very impressed by the speech. He asked the Muslims to recite the Quran. They recited some verses from *Surah Maryam* 19:1-36 about the birth of Yahya(A) and Isa(R). The king was very moved. He refused to surrender the Muslims to *Kuffar*. They were very disappointed. The *Kuffar* held consultations at night. They knew how the teachings of Islam about Isa (A) and his mission are different from the Christian doctrines. So they decided to inform the king of the Muslims' belief about Isa (A). They hoped this way the king will become disillusioned with Muslims and will expell them.

The next day the Makkan leaders again went to King Najashi and told him, "The Muslims do not believe in the divinity of Jesus and have very different ideas about the Christian doctrines."

The king invited the Muslims once again. Jafar (R) presented the Muslims' position on the status of Jesus in Islam thus, "Rasulullah has taught us that Jesus is a servant of God and His messenger. His spirit and His word breathed into virgin Mary."

The king was very impressed with Rasulullah's teachings. He replied, "We believe the same. Blessed be you and your Prophet."

He asked the *Kuffar* to leave his kingdom and promised the Muslims safety under his protection.

The king watched the Muslims and saw how different they were from other Makkans. Slowly he became convinced of the truth of Islam. After some time, he himself became a Muslim. Later, more Muslims went to Abyssinia. In all, eighty-three Muslims are reported to have migrated to Abyssinia.

Points of review:

1. The *Kuffar* persecuted the Muslims and Rasulullah (S) for their faith.
2. Many Muslims migrated to Abyssinia to seek refuge.
2. The *Kuffar* followed the Muslims to Abyssinia but the king of Abyssinia, Najashi, gave refuge to the Muslims, and he himself accepted Islam.

Words to remember

Ahl al-Kitab, disillusion, pagan-faith, plea, refuge, under-privileged.

Important names

Abu Fukaiha (R), Abu Jahl, Abu Lahab, Ammar (R), Bilal (R), Jafar (R), Khabbab(R), King Najashi, Suhaib (R), Sumayyah(R), Yassir(R).

Quranic Study

Read *Surah Maryam* 19:16-35. See how the Quran describes the birth of Isa(A). In what way does this description differ from the Christian doctrines of the "divinity of Christ."

LESSON 10

HAMZAH AND UMAR ACCEPT ISLAM

Sixth Year of Prophethood

Rasulullah's uncle, Hamzah, was only two years older than he was. Hamzah had close, friendly relations with his nephew. Hamzah was a powerful man. He enjoyed hunting and sports. He loved Muhammad (S) but did not seriously think of accepting Islam.

Once, Abu Jahl, the great enemy of Islam, insulted Rasulullah (S). When Hamzah heard of Abu Jahl's behaviour be became furious. He said to himself, "If Muhammad is right, I must support him." He first went to Abu Jahl and warned him to behave in the future. He then went to Rasulullah (S) and accepted Islam. Hamzah was very influential in Makkah and was a courageous person. The Prophet (S) was delighted by Hamzah's conversion to Islam.

Umar was another important covert to Islam. He was an archenemy of Islam. He was an important Arab leader, known for his fearlessness and courage. He also had an uncontrollable temper. Rasulullah (S) knew the weaknesses of Umar but he appreciated his great qualities and knew how that could be used for the cause of Islam. He prayed to Allah, "O Allah, help the cause of Islam through Umar, son of al-Khattab."

Umar had an intense dislike for Rasulullah (S) and his mission. Although other *Kuffar* would not dare to kill Rasulullah(S), Umar decided to kill him by himself.

He came out of his house with a sword in his hand. On his way, he learned that his sister and brother-in-law had become Muslims. He got so angry that he went to their house to teach them a lesson. When Umar reached their house, they, with another *Sahabi*, were reciting the Quran. When they learned that Umar had come they hid the Quran and their friend the *Sahabi*.

Umar was so enraged that he went inside the house and started whipping both his brother-in-law and his sister. Both of them were bleeding but kept on saying, "Yes, we are Muslims. You may kill us, but we shall never give up Islam."

Umar got tired of beating them. He was also impressed by their faith. He decided to listen to the Quran. His sister told him that the Quran is the holy word of Allah. Umar had to clean himself first before reading the Quran. Umar now wanted so much to know about the teachings of the Quran that he agreed to take a bath. The bath not only made Umar's body clean but prepared his heart to receive Allah's guidance. His brother-in-law recited *Surah TaHa*.

When Umar heard the Quran, his heart trembled with fear. He knew it was not a human creation. Its language was perfect and its teachings were pure. When he heard the verse, "Lo, I indeed, I alone am Allah, there is no god except Me, so serve Me," Umar could resist the power of Quran no more. He cried aloud, "It is not man-made. It is perfect and beautiful."

When the *Sahabi* who was hiding heard these words his heart jumped with joy. He came out of hiding running. "Congratulations Umar," he said. "I have heard Rasulullah (S) pray to Allah for your faith."

Umar said, *"La ilaha illa Allah"* and accepted Islam.

Umar now wanted to go to Rasulullah (S) and declare his faith openly. So from there he went straight to the house of Arqam, a *Sahabi* of Rasulullah(S). This house was used by Rasulullah (S) as a school for teaching Islam. This small house was, in fact, the first university of Islam.

As Umar approached the house his sword was still in his hand. When the *Sahabah(R)* saw him coming, they feared trouble. The newly converted Hamzah(R) said, "Let him come. If his intention is not good, I will remove his head from his body with his own sword."

Rasulullah (S) could see the change of heart in Umar. He received Umar with affection and said, "What is your intention, O Umar !"

He replied, "My intention is to accept Islam, O Rasulullah!"

All the Muslims were pleased. Umar said *Shahadah* and accepted Islam.

Umar (R) was a very strong and influential person. His support strengthened the ranks of Muslims. Rasulullah (S) called him *al-Faruq*, the one who distinguishes between the truth and falsehood. Umar al-Faruq later became the second *Khalifah* of Islam. Hamzah (R) died in the battle of Uhud fighting for the cause of Allah.

With Hamzah (R) and Umar (R) in the ranks of Islam, the Muslims felt secure. They declared, "We shall offer our *Salat* in Kabah openly." Hamzah (R) and Umar (R) led the party of Muslims to Kabah and offered *Salat* openly. the *Kuffar* were enraged and attacked the Muslims. But now the Muslims could fight back. The *Kuffar* finally had to accept the rights of Muslims to worship Allah in the Kabah.

Points of Review:

1. Hamzah (R) and Umar (R) accepted Islam.
2. Now the ranks of the Muslims were greatly strengthened.
3. Hamzah (R) and Umar (R) led the Muslims to Kabah and offered *Salat* openly.

Words to remember:

al-Faruq, Khalifah, Shahadah

Important names

Abu Jahl, Hamzah (R), Umar al-Faruq (R)

Quranic Study

Read *Surah TaHa* 20:1-14. What is the message which made the heart of Umar (R) tremble?

LESSON 11

KUFFAR'S OFFER REJECTED
MUSLIMS' SOCIAL BOYCOTT BEGINS

Seventh to Tenth Year of Prophethood

The acceptance of Islam by Hamzah (R) and Umar (R) made the *Kuffar* very nervous. Also, the number of Muslims continued to increase. It was no longer safe for the *Kuffar* to harm and insult Rasulullah (S). They asked the Prophet's family to disown him. But his uncle, Abu Talib, stood firmly with Rasulullah (S).

Some *Kuffar* foolishly thought that Muhammad (S) opposed their religion because he wanted to be their leader. Some of them said, "If we make Muhammad our leader, he will be satisfied. He will not oppose our gods." So they decided to send 'Utba bin Rabi'a, one of their leaders, to Rasulullah (S) to make a generous offer.

Utba went to Rasulullah (S) and told him, "Muhammad, you belong to the noble family of Quraish, but your teachings are destroying our unity. We shall give you everything you want. But we love our idols. Please do not condemn them."

The Prophet (S) listened to him quietly and then replied to them, "I do not do anything for myself. I do not seek any reward from you. My reward is with Allah."

He then recited some verses of the *Surah Ha Mim al-Saidah* to him. :"Ha-Mim: A revelation from the Mercy-giving, the Merciful. It is a book in which verses are explained, a recitation in Arabic for a people who have knowledge." (41:1-3).

'Utba listened to him intently. Rasulullah (S) saw how impressed 'Utba was. He continued to recite, and 'Utba continued to listen for some time. When Rasulullah(S) reached the *Ayah* of *Sajdah*(38). Rasulullah(S) went in *Sajdah*. Then he raised his head from *Sajdah* and said, "This is my answer to your offer. Now you can inform this to your friends."

'Utba got up, went to the chiefs of the Quraish, and told them, "Today I have heard those things which I did not hear before. I advise you not to bother Muhammad."

The chiefs were very disappointed. They said, "Muhammad's magic has affected 'Utba's mind." The *Kuffar* were disappointed, but now they decided on something new and more fearsome. They decided to boycott the Prophet's family, the Banu Hashim.

Banu Hashim were forced to live for three years in a lonely place called the Valley of Abu Talib. The Makkan leaders used their influence to make both the Makkan people and outsiders boycott the Banu Hashim. No one was allowed to visit them or help them. They were deprived of food and water. The Muslims and the family of Rasulullah (S) were hungry and thirsty, but they would not give up.

After three years, the *Kuffar* got tired. They saw that the Muslims loved their religion and would not submit to force. Some *Kuffar* favored ending the boycott.

Three years of hardhips had affected the health of many of the Muslims. Rasulullah's wife, Khadijah (R), and uncle, Abu Talib, were old. They had suffered so much in the valley that they became sick and died soon after their release. Both of them had supported Rasulullah (S) in the most difficult times, and he loved them. Rasulullah (S) was very grieved at this loss.

Khadijah(R) was an example of a good, devoted Muslim wife. Rasulullah(S) had three sons and four daughters with Khadijah(R). His three sons, Qasim(R), Tayyib(R), and Tahir(R), died when they were very young, but the four daughters, Zainab(R), Ruqayyah(R), Umm Kulthum(R), and Fatimah(R), survived. All four of them were married; three of them died in the life-time of Rasulullah(S).

Rasulullah (S) never forgot Khadijah's love and affection, and he remembered her always. Their twenty-five years of life together were an ideal husband and wife relationlship. In Arabia, polygamy was common, and Islam permits it, but Rasulullah(S) did not take a second wife while Khadijah(R) was alive. Thus, he set an example of a monogamous marriage. After her death, Rasulullah(S) married several times and set an example for an ideal polygamous relationship.

Abu Talib never accepted Islam, but he loved his nephew. When all the Makkans were against Muhammad (S), he did not desert him. Rasulullah (S) called it a year of sorrow. Allah once again showed to Muhammad (S) that he must rely on Allah alone and that all human relationships are, in fact, temporary.

Points of review:

1. The *Kuffar* tried to tempt Rasulullah (S) but they were disappointed.
2. They made a social boycott of Rasulullah's family for three years.

---

[1] According to some accounts Rasulullah(S) had only one son, Ibrahim(R) from Khadijah(R); Tayyib(R) and Tahir(R) were his titles.

3. Rasulullah (S) lost his wife, Khadijah (R), and uncle Abu Talib, due to the hardhips of the social boycott.

Words to remember:

Boycott, fearsome.

Important names

Utba bin Rabi'a, Valley of Abu Talib.

Quranic Study

Read *Ha Mim Sajdah* 41:1-38. What does it say about: 1) The Quran; 2) Prophet Muhammad's mission; 3) Powers of Allah; 4) and the *Kuffar?*

LESSON 12

OPPOSITION OF THE KUFFAR

The Quran says that Allah helps those people who seek the truth to find it. But those who see the truth and reject it, Allah confirms them in their disbelief and disobedience. The *Kuffar* of Makkah who were not convinced of the truth of Rasulullah's mission by his pure life, his plain message of the Quran, and the noble teachings of Islam tried hard to find excuses for not believing in Rasulullah (S). They placed obstinate demands upon him to prove his truthfulness. They spread all kinds of false propaganda against him.

The *Kuffar* could very well see that the Quran was a unique piece of literature which could not be imitated. The poets among the Arabs had very high status, but Muhammad (S) had never shown any poetic talent. When the *Kuffar* heard the *Wahi* in its most beautiful and perfect language, they were hard pressed to explain how an illiterate person could, all of a sudden, produce such knowledge. Many of them immediately thought that Muhammad (S) had become poet. But there is a great difference between poetic compositions and the message of the Quran. And the life of Rasulullah (S) was in sharp contrast to the life of poets. Allah refutes that charge. "We have not taught him poetry nor poetry is worthy of him." *(Ya Sin 36:69)*

The *Kuffar* should have known the difference between poetry and revelation. A poet uses only his imagination. His thoughts are stray and random and he rarely writes to deliver a message.

There is also a great difference between a poet's words and deeds. The Quran says, "And how the poets say what they do not do." *(al-Shu'ara' 26:226)*

Rasulullah (S) was, on the other hand, a practical teacher. His life was the teachings of the Quran in practice. Besides, the Quran was a divine message for all mankind, and very different from any composition of poetry. The *Kuffar* should have understood that.

Many *Kuffar* were not convinced that Muhammad (S) had all of a sudden become a poet. They needed some other explanation. They declared that Muhammad (S) was possessed by the *jinns* (genies) and spirits.

They were not thinking very clearly. Evil spirits do not have the noble purpose of guiding mankind to its creator. How can a man under the control of evil spirits act in noble way or deliver a coherent and pure message? The Quran said, "Shall I tell you upon whom the devils descend? They descend on every sinful and false person." (al-Shu'ara' 26:221-23).

Even the enemies of Islam knew that Muhammad (S) was noble, honest, and truthful. It should also be obvious to every reasonable person that people possessed by spirits are incoherent and inconsistent. They have no message to deliver. The Quran talked about the stupidity of the *Kuffar*:

> Don't the *Kuffar* think that their friend (Muhammad) is not in any
> way under the influence of *Jinns*. Indeed! He is a plain warner
> (to the evil doers). *al-A'raf* 7:184

Some people had different ideas about messengers. They felt that Allah would not choose a human being for His cause. They expected at least an angel. They did not understand that an angel could not become a model for human actions. In Rasulullah (S) Allah created a human model for us to follow.

In the Arab mind, a prophet should be a supernatural being. Therefore, they ridiculed Rasulullah(S) by saying, "What kind of messenger is he, that he eats food and walks on the street." (al-Furqan 25:7). They expected the Prophet (S) to be accompanied by visible angels. Special gardens should grow to feed him, and God should offer him treasures to be distributed among the people. (See *al-Furqan* 25:8). The *Kuffar* were not prepared to receive the message; therefore, they were not ready to accept the role of the Prophet (S) as a model teacher.

The message of the Quran and authentic information it contained of the past events, made some people think how Muhammad (S) could all of a sudden become knowledgable about unknown things. But they were not prepared to accept this sudden outpouring of knowledge in a most beautiful language as a proof of his prophethood. Therefore, they charged, "Only a man teaches him." (al-Nahl 16:103).

The *Kuffar* even mentioned the names of some foreign born slaves as teachers of Muhammad(S). They had accepted Islam but were still under the ownership of the *Kuffar*. The Quran refutes the charge of the *Kuffar*, "the speech of him whom the *Kuffar* refer is foreign and the Quran is in clear Arabic speech." (al-Nahl 16:103).

Some *Kuffar* went so far as to accuse Rasulullah(S) of inventing lies. "Those who disbelieve say," the Quran declared, "this is nothing but a lie which he has invented, and other people have helped him in it." *(al-Furqan 25:4)*. Allah defended Rasulullah (S) from all such accusations, confirming, "He (Allah), who knows the secret of heavens and those of the earth, has revealed it." *(al-Furqan 25:6)*

In fact, all these accusations of the *Kuffar* have no basis. They themselves were not convinced of their rationality. But they disbelieved, so they wanted some explanation of the miraculous nature of the Quran and Rasulullah's source of true information. They also wanted to convince people not to accept Rasulullah's message. This propaganda did play a role in keeping many people away from Rasulullah (S). However, his charming personality, his sincerity, and the power of the words of the Quran were such that many people decided to meet him and hear the Quran. Whoever did so with an open mind became convinced of the truth of his mission and accepted Islam.

In a later chapter we shall deal in detail with the real causes of *Kuffars'* refusal to accept Muhammad (S) as Allah's messenger and prophet.

Points of review:

1. The *Kuffar* opposed Rasulullah (S) by placing obstinate demands upon him.

2. The *Kuffar* thought that Rasulullah (S) had become a poet or was possessed by *Jinns*, that someone else was teaching him, or that he himself was inventing lies.

3. In the Quran, Allah defended His prophet from all such accusations.

Words to remember:
Jinns, obstinate, propaganda, rationality, unique.

Quranic Study

We have quoted many verses to show the *Kuffar's* accusations and Allah's defense of Rasulullah's mission. Find these verses in the Quran and see how the Quran presents these arguments. Write Quran's arguments in support of Rasulullah (S) in your own words.

LESSON 13

FAILURE IN TAIF

Tenth and Eleventh Year of Prophethood

Opposition continued in Makkah, so Rasulullah(S) decided to go and preach in another city, Ta'if. Ta'if was the center of the tribes of Thaqif and Hawazin. It housed the temple of their god, al-Lat. It is located on an elevated plain, and rich Makkans used it as a summer resort.

Rasulullah (S) went there with Zaid (R), his adopted son and freed slave. The people of Taif proved to be worse than the Makkan *Kuffar*. They were a rich and proud people, who firmly believed in their gods.

When Rasulullah (S) met the leaders of Thaqif and invited them to Islam, they ridiculed him and pelted him with stones. He was bodily injured. He was bleeding all over. Zaid (R) was also hit on his head and was bleeding. Young boys made fun of Rasulullah (S) and chased him out of town. But he did not curse them or lose heart.

Rasulullah (S) had been informed by Allah earlier that rich and proud people have always rejected their prophets. The Quran says,

> We have not sent to any town a warner
> but its proud inhabitants declare, "We shall
> not believe in the revelation which you bring."

> And they say, 'We have plenty of wealth and lots of
> children. We shall not be punished.
> *Saba* 34:34-35

Rasulullah's mission was to invite mankind to the right path and save them from Hell. In this task he knew that only Allah would help him.

Outside of Taif he sat to rest in a garden near a vineyard. He reflected on the happenings of the day, then looked up to heaven. He raised his hands and prayed,

> O, Allah, to You alone I make complaint
> of my helplessness, lack of resources
> and insignificance before other men.
>
> You are most Merciful. The Lord
> of the helpless and You are my Lord.
>
> In whose hands would You abandon me —
> of an unsympathetic enemy and an unkind
> foe? But if You are not angry with me
> I don't worry about anything else.
>
> I seek protection in the Light of Your
> face. You alone control all affairs
> of this world as well as of the
> hereafter. And there is no power
> except Your power.

These noble sentiments of Rasulullah(S) must have moved the Heaven. Allah knew very well the suffering of His prophet, and He alone knew the great rewards of the future.

Allah sent an angel to Rasulullah(S) who told Rasulullah(S), "If you wish, Allah will unite the two mountains on both sides of Taif and crush the people between them."

Rasulullah (S), who was sent as a mercy for all mankind, replied to the angel, "No! I don't want any punishment for them. I hope Allah will guide them and their children to the straight path of Islam."

Allah, in fact, heard the prayers of Rasulullah(S) and fulfilled his desire; ten years later the tribes of Hawazin and Thaqif accepted Islam.

As Rasulullah (S) and Zaid (R) sat by the vineyards, its owner saw them. He was moved to see their condition. As a gesture of Arab hospitality, he sent them a gift of grapes through his salve, Addas. Rasulullah (S) accepted the gift, saying, "*Bismi Allah al-Rahman al-Rahim.* (in the name of Allah the Mercy-giving, the Merciful.)"

This form of acceptance surprised Addas. He said, "These words are not generally spoken by people here." Rasulullah(S) asked him where he came from. Addas replied, "I am a Christian from Nineveh." Rasulullah (S) was pleased to hear this. He said, "Oh you are from the city of my brother Yunus (A), the prophet of Allah."

A conversation with Rasulullah (S) convinced Addas of the truth of Rasulullah's mission. He kissed Rasulullah's hands and became a Muslim. He helped the injured Prophet (S) take a good rest.

When the masters of Addas learned about this they became furious. They warned him about the serious consequences of this act. But Addas had seen the truth. He bravely replied, "No one living on earth today is better than this Prophet. He has told me a truth which only a prophet could tell."

The news of the unsuccessful mission of Rasulullah (S) delighted the Makkans. It emboldened them to persecute Rasulullah(S) and his companions even more. But Allah had decided to greatly honor His Prophet and through him to honor his *ummah*.

Points of review:

1. Rasulullah (S) with Zaid (R) went to Taif to preach Islam.
2. The people of Taif rejected the Prophet's call, insulted him and injured him.
3. Rasulullah (S) turned to Allah and prayed for His mercy and help.

Words to remember:

Consequences, embolden, foe, insignificance.

Important names

Addas (R), al-Lat, Hawazin, Taif, Thaqif.

Quranic Study

The name of Prophet Yunus is mentioned in several verses of the Quran (*al-Nisa'* 4:163; *al-An'am* 6: 86; *Yunus* 10:98.

Surah al-Saffat 37:139-147 briefly narrates his story. Read it with the help of a *Tafsir*.

Dome of the Rock

Interior view of the Dome of the Rock from where Rasulullah Ascended to the Heavens.

LESSON 14

ISRA' AND MI'RAJ: JOURNEY TO AL-QUDS (JERUSALEM) AND ASCENSION TO HEAVEN

Twelfth Year of Prophethood

Allah had seen how Rasulullah (S) worked hard for Islam. He suffered much but he never complained. In fact, he always thanked Allah for the honor of serving Islam and doing Allah's will. Whenever he was not preaching or teaching his companions, he was saying his *Salat* and reciting the Quran. He also spent long hours at night saying *Salat*.

Now Allah decided to honor his last prophet by inviting him to visit Heaven and show Muhammad (S) His signs. Jibril (A) one night came to Rasulullah (S), woke him from his sleep and invited him to visit Heaven. He offered Rasulullah (S) a Buruq, a heavenly animal with wings, to serve as his ride. Jibril (A) took him first to Kabah. He opened Rasulullah's chest and washed his heart with the pure water of Zamzam. He then filled his heart with *Nur*, the divine light of faith and wisdom. Rasulullah (S) needed special preparation because he was going to be received by Allah. From Kabah, Jibril (A) and Rasulullah (S) went to the *Masjid al-Aqsa* in Al-Quds (Jerusalem). This *Masjid* was first built by Prophet Da'wud (A). It was completed by his son, Prophet Sulaiman (A). It had been destroyed by the Romans. Prophet Muhammad (S) prayed on the site of the *Masjid*.

This *Masjid* is the third holiest place of Islam. It also served as a direction of *Qiblah* for the Muslims in the early Islamic period. *Khalifah* Umar (R) built a *Masjid* at that site. The beautiful Dome of Rock was later built exactly on the site from where Rasulullah (S) ascended to heaven.

From the rock in the *Masjid*, Buraq took Rasulullah (S) to Heaven. In Paradise, Rasulullah (S) met all the prophets. Wherever he went, he was greeted very warmly. He saw both Paradise and Hell. Then he went to the highest Heaven. *Sidrat al Muntaha*, where no angels or human beings could go. This is the closest point to *Arsh*, the seat of Allah's power and majesty. Allah spoke to Muhammad (S) directly.

Through Rasulullal (S) Allah wanted the Muslim *Ummah* (Community) to be closer to him. So Allah made five daily *Salats* obligatory for all Muslims. *Salat* is described by Rasulullah (S) as *Miraj* (ascension) for the Muslims." In our *Salat* we stand face to face with Allah and speak to Him directly. Thanks to the gift of *Salat* the Muslims do not need priests to plead to Allah on their behalf.

Allah also honored Rasulullah (S) by giving him two more gifts. One of them was the last two verses of *Surah al-Baqarah*. The first verse deals with the faith of Muslims, and the second verse teaches a beautiful invocation to Allah for His help.

The second gift was the promise of Allah that the period of long suffering was about to end and a new era was about to begin.

After a visit to all the Heavens, Buraq brought Rasulullah (S) back to the *Masjid al-Aqsa*. All the prophets were waiting for him there. He led a prayer as their *Imam* (the leader). From the *Masjid al-Aqsa*, he returned home. All this travel took him a very short time. His bed was warm, and the chain on the door was still swinging. It was indeed a great miracle. In honoring His last prophet, Allah has honored us all and promised us His forgiveness.

The next morning, Rasulullah (S) told this story to all the Makkans. Those who believed in him knew that Allah who sends Jibril (A) with *Wahi* had indeed honored His prophet. The *Kuffar* thought of it as another unbelievable claim of Muhammad (S). They found in it another reason to make fun of the Prophet (S). The Muslims, however, told this story to each other and thanked Allah for His kindness to their Prophet (S) and to the entire Muslim *Ummah*.

Muslims in thankfulness to Allah ever since have maintained five daily *Salats*. *Salat* is the second *Rukn* (pillar) of Islam. It establishes closest relationship between us and our Creator and Lord.

Points of review:

1. Rasulullah's mission to Taif ended in failure.

2. Allah honored His prophet by inviting him to Heaven.

3. Allah honored Rasulullah's *Ummah* by the gift of five daily *Salat*.

Words to remember:

Imam, Mi'raj, Nur, Qiblah.

Important names:

Buraq, Zaid.

Quranic Study:

1. Read and memorise the last two verses of *Surah al-Baqarah* 2:285-286.

2. Read *Surah al-Isra' (Bani Isra'il)* 17:1. What is the purpose of Rasul Allah's night journeys described here?

3. *Surah al-Isra'* belongs to the last phase of Makkan life. It has important message for the future course the Muslim *Ummah* was going to take in Madinah. Study some of these aspects of this *Surah:*

   i. The Jews, because of their continuous disobedience have been dismissed from their role as chosen people. Acceptance of Islam can once again offer them a chance. (17:3-9)

   ii. *Kuffar* are given final warning for the evil consequence of their disbelief. (17:16-18, 41)

   iii. The moral foundation of Muslim polity (see Lesson 18 *Quranic Study*).

LESSON 15

SUCCESS IN YATHRIB (MADINAH)
Tenth, Eleventh and Twelfth Years of Prophethood

The event of *Mi'raj* strengthened the faith of the Muslims. The Quran told them that the time for the fulfillment of Allah's promises was very near. The faith and confidence of Muslims irritated the *Kuffar*. All their efforts to stop the progress of Islam had failed. Now they were seriously considering killing Rasulullah (S).

The risk of the life of Rasulullah (S) was increasing. He was not afraid at all. He knew Allah had appointed him to complete His mission. He must do what Allah wanted him to do. His failure at Makkah and Ta'if did not discourage Rasululah (S). He made renewed efforts in another direction.

It was the habit of Rasulullah (S) to go to assemblies and fairs to invite people to Islam. The Arabs gathered in Makkah each year for a pilgrimage. A group of six pilgrims from Yathrib (the city now known as Madinah) came for pilgrimage. They belonged to the important tribe of Khazraj.

The people of Khazraj had known about a coming prophet. Many Jewish tribes lived in Yathrib. They followed Prophet Musa (A) and read *Tawrat* (Torah), the book revealed to Prophet Musa (A) by Allah. This book told them about a prophet who would come and bring peace to mankind. The people of Yathrib had learned from the Jews about the coming prophet for whom the Jews were eagerly waiting.

At the time of pilgrimage, Prophet Muhammad (S) met the people of Khazraj and invited them to Islam. Unlike the people of Makkah and Ta'if, the people of Yathrib listened to Rasulullah (S) with respect. The teachings of the Quran and sincerity of Rasulullah (S) convinced them that he was the prophet foretold in the *Tawrat*. "If Muhammad was a true prophet," they thought, "then we should be the first to accept him before the Jews recognised him."

Rasulullah (S) read them some portions of the Quran. They were convinced that Muhammad (S) was a true prophet. The Quran was divine revelation, and Islam was a true religion. All of them said, *"La ilaha illa Allah Muhammadun Rasulullah"* and became Muslims.

They told Rasulullah (S), "Our people are most divided. Maybe Allah will unite them through you." This was the beginning of a big success. Allah's promises on the night of *Mi'raj* began to be fulfilled.

These people went back to Yathrib and told their brothers about the pious Prophet (S) and his pure religion, Islam. Many more people became interested. People of Madinah saw that the lives of their brothers from Khazraj tribe had completely changed since they had accepted Islam. Now all their actions were different from their actions in earlier pagan life. The interest of the people of Madinah in learning more about Islam and knowing more about the Prophet (S) increased.

The next year, twelve pilgrims came to Makkah especially to meet Rasulullah (S). They met the Prophet (S) and listened to the Quran. They also became Muslims. Rasulullah (S) took *Bai'ah* (formal oath or pledge) from them. He asked them to promise:

> To worship only one God;
> not to steal,
> not to commit adultery,
> not to kill their children,
> not to make false allegation
> against others,
> and to faithfully follow the
> teachings of Islam.

This *Bai'ah* is called the first pledge of 'Aqaba. 'Aqaba is a mount near Makkah.

This time Rasulullah(S) sent two *Sahabah*, Mus'ab bin 'Umar and 'Abdullah bin Ummi Maktum to Yathrib with them. These companions started teaching Islam to the people of Yathrib. More and more people listened and became interested in Islam. The message of Islam reached everyone in Madinah. The next year, seventy-two Muslims, including two women, came for pilgrimage and to meet Rasulullah (S). These Muslims were so happy to see Rasulullah (S) they told him, "O' Rasulullah, we have come to listen to you and obey you. We believe in you and shall always stand by you."

Rasulullah (S) was very happy. He taught them what Islam means. He recited some of the Quran to them. These people became even more convinced of the truth of Muhammad's prophethood. They made a promise to always believe in Islam and to stand by the Prophet (S) and defend him.

Rasulullah (S) was pleased by this devotion and faith. He in return promised them to stand by them always, in life as well as in death. The people of Yathrib wanted a formal *Bai'ah*. As Rasulullah(S) was about to invite them for *Bai'ah*, Abbas bin 'Ubadah asked the people, "Do you know what *Bai'ah* means?" He paused a little, then continued, "It is a declaration of war with both the Arabs and non-Arabs."

All the members of the delegation replied, "Yes, we know it indeed. We shall keep our pledge even at the cost of our lives."

All the members of the Yathrib delegation stretched their hands for *Bai'ah* and promised,
>We shall obey Rasulullah
>in plenty and scarcity,
>in ease and difficulties,
>in joy and sorrow.
>We will serve the cause of Allah
>under all situations.

Rasulullah (S) said,
>My blood is your blood.
>I am of you, you are of me.

Rasulullah (S) called the people of Yathrib *Ansar*, the helpers to the cause of Allah. Being the *Sahabah* of Allah's last prophet made the people of Yathrib very happy and filled their hearts with joy. They wished Rasulullah (S) to live with them. They now wanted an opportunity to serve Rasulullah (S) and Islam. All of them knew the dangers to their lives if Muhammad (S) and the Muslims went to live with them. But faith had entered their hearts. Risking their lives for Islam didn't appear dangerous to them, but very attractive.

They invited Rasulullah (S) and other persecuted Muslim brothers to migrate to Yathrib. They promised to help them. "Even if all the Arabs and non-Arabs unite against us," they said, "we shall support Rasulullah and be faithful to the cause of Allah."

Rasulullah (S) knew and respected their sincerity and pure faith. He honored them and called them *Ansar* (singular, *Ansari*), the helpers of Allah. The people of Yathrib were greatly delighted by this title. People of Yathrib were known by this name. They, in fact, showed in the future how correct this honor was.

Rasulullah (S) was not yet asked by Allah to migrate. He stayed in Makkah but he asked Muslims to migrate to Yathrib.

Muslims slowly started migrating to Yathrib, where they were warmly received. Through *Tabligh* (preaching) Islam started spreading fast in Madinah.

Points of review:

1. At 'Aqaba, delegations from Yathrib took *Bai'ah* of obedience to Rasulullah (S).
2. The message of Islam was accepted by many people of Yathrib.
3. Rasulullah (S) called the Muslims of Yathrib *Ansar*.

Words to remember:

Allegation, *Ansar, Ansari, Bai'ah, Tabligh*

Important names

'Abbas bin 'Ubadah, 'Abdullah bin Ummi Maktum, 'Aqaba, Khazraj, Mus'ab bin 'Umair.

Quranic Study

1. Read *al-Anfal* 62-63, *Ali Imran* 3:102-105. See How Allah united the hearts of a divided people through faith.

LESSON 16

WHY KUFFAR DID NOT BELIEVE IN RASULULLAH (S)

Rasulullah's call to Islam was accepted by some Makkans who became his *Sahabah* and served the cause of Allah. Their faith in Islam and dedication to Rasulullah (S) made them undergo severe hardships, but they never gave up Islam. The *Kuffar* on the other hand remained confirmed in their false beliefs and continued to work against the cause of Islam. In the next two chapters we shall analyse the reasons for the attitude of both these groups.

First, let us look at the *Kuffar!*

Rasulullah (S) was well known in Makkah for his righteousness. He was known as *al-Sadiq* and *al-Amin*. He was supported by the miracle of Quran. Everyone recognized that the Quran was not written by a human being. The teachings of Islam were noble and pure. Still the *Kuffar* opposed Rasulullah (S).

The Quran says that only those people who want to discover the truth can find it. Allah gives His guidance to those who fear Him and seek guidance from Him (*al-Baqarah* 2:1-5). But Allah hardens the hearts of those who reject the truth and oppose it, and makes them "deaf, dumb and blind"(*al-Baqarah* 2:7) to truth. Thus, in Makkah, some people searched for the truth and found it. Most Makkans opposed it and became its worst enemy, and Allah confirmed them in their *Kufr* because of their obstinacy.

There are some other reasons also that we may discuss here. It is true that Rasulullah's teachings were good for all mankind. But the *Kuffar* feared that it would bring an end to their economic well being, their free way of life and their superior social status. It was not easy for them to give up the way of life of their ancestors. It guaranteed them benefits and pleasures in this world instead of promises of paradise.

In the Quran we read their answer, "When it is said to them Come to that which Allah has revealed and to the messenger,' they reply, 'Enough for us is this way of life on which we found our ancestors." (*al-Ma'idah* 5:104). Thus it is always difficult for most people to change when it affects their personal benefits.

Rasulullah(S) taught that Allah is One. The *Kuffar* had many gods and goddesses. Their fathers and grandfathers had worshipped these gods for generations. The *Kuffar* were very attached to them. It was not easy to give up their beliefs in idols, even though some of the *Kuffar* knew that the idols, in fact, had no power.

The *Kuffar* drew economic benefits from their religious beliefs which they feared they might lose by becoming Muslims. Makkah was the center of Arab religion. Quraish were in charge of Kabah. Kabah had three hundred and sixty-five idols. People came from all over Arabia to worship these idols in Kabah. The Makkans made a lot of money through these pilgrims. "If Muhammad succeeds," they thought, "that would be the end of our money-making religion." The love of wealth and the greed for money prevents many people from following the truth. And this was a serious factor in the Makkan's refusal to accept Islam.

Islam also challenged their free way of life and invited them to a responsible and righteous life. The Quraish were smart businessmen. To make money by all methods, fair or foul, was their way of life. Thus, cheating in business was very common. They feared that Islamic principles of honesty in business dealings would destroy their wealth.

The leaders of the Quraish were also very greedy. Islam's call for social justice, charity, and human equality was not appreciated by the pleasure seeking Quraish. If one of their relatives died, and they were to take care of his children or wives, they would steal his wealth. They treated his family as they wished. We have already seen how harsh they were even to their old parents. They had no respect for women. It was a matter of shame to have daughters, so many Arabs killed their daughters to save themselves from embarrassment. There was a lot of slave trading in those days, and slaves were treated like animals; they had no respect and no rights.

Believing themselves superior to all other people, the Quraish thought they could behave as they wished. So they went around gambling, drinking, killing, cheating and exploiting other people for their own benefit.

The *Kuffar* never wanted to be responsible to Allah and change their way of life. in the Makkan period the central message of Islam was Tawhid, Oneness of Allah, and Akhirah, the Day of Judgement. Both these points went against the religious and social view of Quraish. By denying *Akhirah* they denied their moral responsibility in this life.

For many *Kuffar* it was more difficult to believe in the person of Muhammad (S). He (S) was an orphan and a poor person. They believed Allah should have chosen His prophet from among the rich and powerful chiefs of Makkah or Taif. The Quran speaks about the objection of the *Kuffar*. "If only this Quran was revealed to some great man of the two towns." (*al-Zukhruf* 43:31). They didn't understand that prophethood is Allah's choice, and Islam does not recognize anyone's birthrights or status because of his color, race, social origin, or wealth.

Some of them had strange ideas about prophethood. They thought a prophet should not be a human being, or that he should descend from heaven with a host of angels. The prophet, they thought, should perform miracles instead of teaching good things. They were familiar with some of the stories of the miracles of the prophets in the past. Therefore, many *Kuffar* demanded,

> And the *Kuffar* say:
> We shall not believe in you till you
> cause a spring to come forth out of earth,
> or until you haul a garden of palm and wine,
> and you cause in the middle of it a river to come out,
> or until you cause the heavens to fall
> upon us as pieces as you have told us,
> or you produce God and angels ascending
> or until you have a house decorated with
> gold, or you ascend into heaven.
> Nor we shall believe in your ascent
> unless you bring down to us a writing
> which we may read.
> *al-Isra'* 17:90-93

The Quran replied to all these demands in the most simple way,
> Say (O Muhammad to the *Kuffar*), Glorified
> be my Lord, I am but a human messenger.
> *al-Isra'* 17-93

Allah did not send Rasulullah (S) as a wonder worker but as a moral teacher. Though Rasulullah (S) performed many miracles, the emphasis of the Quran is on his teachings. In replying to such absurd claims Allah asks Rasulullah (S) to tell the *Kuffar*,

> Say! For myself I have no power to
> benefit, nor power to hurt save that
> what Allah wills. Had I the knowledge
> of the unseen I would have gathered
> for myself abundant wealth, and adversity
> would not touch me. I am but a warner and
> a bearer of good tidings to the people who believe.
> al-A'raf 7:188

The Quran thus explained that the real power in all affairs belongs to Allah and the prophets have only those powers which Allah desires them to have. The miracles of the prophets are a gift from Allah to support them and convince the people. However, miracles were never sufficient proof for the non-believers. They demand miracles, but when they are produced, they called them magical tricks and turned away.

The *Kuffar* did not realize that the aim of all the prophets was to teach Allah's commandments. The prophets show us how we can be pious and good through their actions and not through miracles, or family connections, or wealth.

Islam wanted to bring to an end their beliefs, their idol worship, their pride, their deceit, and their evil ways, but the *Kuffar* were not ready to change. These are some of the reasons why the *Kuffar* opposed Islam and became the enemies of Rasulullah (S).

Many among the Quraish and the Arabs who had accepted Islam were corrupt like their other Arab brothers. But once they became Muslims they were completely changed. Now they knew that Allah is One and they are responsible to Him. They recited the Quran and learned the wisdom they never knew before. They loved Rasulullah (S). They saw in him the best example of a pious, God-fearing, upright, truthful, and honest person. They tried to follow him in their everyday lives.

In spite of all the cruelties of the *Kuffar*, Muslims would not give up their religion, Islam, or their love for Rasulullah (S). Instead, they were prepared to give up their homes, property, relatives, and city. When the Prophet (S) asked them to migrate to Yathrib, they willingly gave up their homes and left for Yathrib.

Points of review:

1. Islam challenged the *Kuffars'* religious beliefs, social status, and free way of life and invited them to a responsible and righteous living.

2. The Arabs who accepted Islam were completely changed in their personal life and social outlook.

3. While the *Kuffar* opposed Rasulullah(S) the faith of the Muslims became more firm.

Words to remember:

Exploit, obstinacy.

Quranic Study

1. In this chapter we have quoted many verses. Look up all these verses in the Quran. Read their meaning with *Tafsir*. Write in your own language about the objections of the *Kuffar* and Allah's defence of His prophet.

2. In this connection you may once again like to read the verses which speak about the *Kuffars'* beliefs and ways of life. See Quranic Study, Lesson I, *Jahiliyyah*.

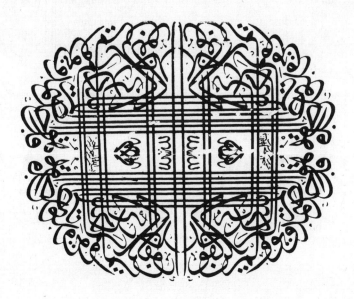

Forms of Bismillah - al-Rahman il-Rahim

By Ahmed Karahisārī, Turkey, 16th cty

From Turkish ms. Lâleli KN 1829, 15th cty, Turkey

In oval shape, 19th cty (a)

From the Quṭub minār, Delhi, beginning 13th cty

In Ta'līq, by Abdulqādir 1351/1932

From the miḥrāb of Sar-i Pul, Afghanistan, 2nd half of 12th century

By Ahmed Karahisārī, Turkey, 16th cty

Muslims developed the fine art of Quranic Calligraphy

LESSON 17

WHY MUSLIMS BELIEVED IN RASULULLAH (S)

Rasulullah's invitation to Islam earned him many enemies, but it also gave him sincere and devoted followers. No prophet or religious leader had, in his life, such a dedicated group of followers.

The number of Rasulullah's *Sahabah* in Makkah was small. This small circle of companions, however, was the most fortunate group in the world. They were early muslims and had an opportunity to spend the longest time with their Prophet (S). They had the full benefit of Rasulullah's blessed company. They underwent hardships, performed great sacrifices, and rendered great services to Islam. Muslims remember them with love and devotion.

Here we ask the question: Why did these early Muslims accept Islam?

For these early Muslims there was no material benefit in accepting Islam. On the other hand, there were many risks. Constant persecution and harassment by the *Kuffar* had made life miserable for small Muslim communities. The weak among them were punished severely. There was an ever present danger to their lives. Some in fact, were even killed by the *Kuffar*. Many were forced to seek sanctuary in Abyssinia. When Rasulullah (S) asked them to leave their country and make hijrah to Madinah they willingly followed their Prophet (S). There must have been some special reason for them to believe in Islam and willingly suffer for their faith.

The very first Muslims were those who knew Rasulullah (S) personally. These people knew his truthfulness, honesty, simplicity, and sincerity, and they were convinced that he could never tell a lie. These people drew even closer to him after they became Muslims. This reputation of honesty and truth also convinced others who did not know him well. Among the early converts were some of those people who initially were not prepared to accept him as a prophet. But when they met him they became convinced of his sincerity and embraced Islam.

His personality must have been extraordinary. Whoever met him was influenced. Before his prophethood he had not looked for leadership. In fact, he retired from the world and sat in the cave of Hira. He never went back to Hira after he became a prophet. All his life became public. Those who accepted Islam remained deeply attached to him.

His *Khulq* (morals and manners) were exemplary. No other human being has shown those traits and character so strongly. A'ishah(R) has said, "Rasulullah's character was the Quran in practice." In Makkah, Rasulullah (S) was persecuted but he remained patient. He was tempted by the *Kuffar* with beautiful offers, but he rejected them. He was kind and loving to his followers and just and considerate to his enemies. He was not provoked to anger when ridiculed and attacked. He never cursed even his worst enemies. In every situation he remained patient and attached to Allah. His days and nights were spent in prayers and *Tabligh* (preaching).

He never desired anything for himself. He did not seek comfort and luxury. Whatever he received he gave away in the way of Allah. He was so deeply religious and so morally perfect — an embodiment of truth, piety and sincerity — that anyone who met him with an open mind became his humble follower.

His *Sahabah (R)* imitated him in all the things they did and followed his instructions in every aspect of their life. After he was dead (May Allah bless his soul) His *Sahabah (R)* followed his *Sunnah* (tradition). *Sunnah* are the acts of the Prophet (S) and his instructions. *Sahabah (R)* and early generations of Muslims wrote down his *Sunnah* and Rasulullah's instructions. All Muslims have ever since tried to follow his *Sunnah*. Thus, both his personality and his character played important part in convincing the Arabs about the truth of his mission.

The revelation of the Quran was also a very important factor in the spread of Islam. Other prophets performed many miracles. Quran is the single most important miracle of Rasulullah(S). Its language is powerful, its style is unique, and its message is pure. Arabs were very proud of their language. They honored their poets and orators. That, perhaps, is the reason why Allah gave the Prophet (S) a miracle which showed such inimitable perfection of language. The language of the Quran was so beautiful that anyone who heard it was convinced of its superhuman character.

They knew that no human being could write that language. Many also knew that Prophet Muhammad (S) was unlettered. He was not known as an orator, a poet or story teller. People knew he could not compose such verses. In fact, all of them agreed that no one could compose such verses. Thus, anyone who heard the Quran without bias was convinced of its truth and became a Muslim.

Among the Arabs there were some people who still believed in one God and followed the teaching of Prophet Ibrahim (A) and Prophet Ismail (A). They were called *Hanif*. They did not like the evil ways of the Arabs. They had heard from Jews and Christians that a prophet is about to come. When they met Rasulullah (S) and heard the Quran, they became convinced of the truth of Rasulullah's mission and became Muslims.

Among the Makkans there were many slaves, widows (and women in general), orphans, and old people who were treated unjustly. Nobody cared about them. The Quran warned the powerful Quraish to stop their evil practices, give up their pride of race and sex, and treat all human beings with justice and human equality. By accepting Islam, these poor and helpless people suffered more, but the acceptance of Islam gave them a new faith and new dignity. They readily suffered but never gave up Islam.

Early Muslims themselves became message bearers of Islam. The acceptance of Islam changed their lives. Love of Allah, love of Rasulullah (S), and their good actions made them fine examples to other human beings. The people who met *Sahabah* became convinced of their true faith and became Muslims themselves.

Thus, not only the personality of Rasulullah (S) but also the character of early Muslims was very important in the spread of Islam. Wherever they went, both inside and outside Arabia, people looked at *Sahabah* and said, "These are the faces of people who speak the truth and practice righteousness." They wanted to be like the Muslims. They also accepted Islam. Islam is a religion for all humanity, and it freely admits all people to its fold. It is in this way that Islam spread fast and became a world force.

The *Sunnah* of Prophet Muhammad(S), the Book of Allah, the message of social equality, and the *Sunnah* of pious Muslims is still before us. If we follow it like early Muslims, Allah and His Prophet(S) will be pleased and the world will follow us. If we give up these things then we shall follow the world and the world will elude us.

Points of review:

1. For early Muslims there were no material benefits for accepting Islam, but there were many risks.

2. Rasulullah's personality, personal characteristics, revelations of the Quran and Islam's social message were important factors in the acceptance of Islam by early Muslims.

2. Acceptance of Islam completely changed the life of the *Sahabah*; and they themselves became exemplary models of Islamic teachings.

Words to remember:

Embrace, *Hanif*, sanctuary, superhuman.

Quranic Study

1. We should study the characteristics of Rasulullah (S) from the Quran and see what Allah says about him.

   Study the following verses and write an estimate of Rasulullah's mission and character.

   His Mission: *al-Fath* 48:8-9
   Gentleness: *ali-'Imran* 3:159
   Mercy: *al-Tawbah* 9:61, *al-Qasas* 28:46
   His Arguments: *al-Nahl* 16:125
   Selflessness: *al-Furqan* 25:57
   His pattern: *al-Ahzab* 33:21
   His Role: *al-Baqarah* 2:151; *al-Ahzab* 33:40-45
   al-Talaq 65:11
   His character: *al-Qalam* 68:4
   His prayer: *al-Muzammil* 73:1-9
   Truthful messenger: *Yunus* 10:12-14
   Patience: *al-Qasas* 28:126-127

2. The Quran is a mircale which could not be produced by human beings. Study the following verses to understand the claim of the Quran.

   al-Baqarah 2:23; *Hud* 11:13
   Yunus 10:38; *al-Kahf* 18:88

LESSON 18

HIJRAH OF RASULULLAH (S)

Thirteenth Year of Prophethood

The news of Islam's success in Yathrib made the *Kuffar* extremely angry. Their leaders met and finally decided to kill Rasulullah (S). But Allah had different plans for him. Allah had first asked him to advise the Muslims to make *Hijrah* quietly to Yathrib. By this example we learn that one's ties to Islam come before his relationships to his country, property, and relatives. Therefore, if Muslims are unable to practice Islam in one place, they are required by Allah to migrate to a country where they can be free.

Hijrah is a very important aspect of Islam. We shall talk about it in more detail in Part II of this book. Allah says in the Quran,"O My servants, indeed My earth is spacious. Therefore serve Me alone." *(al-Ankabut* 29:56). Thus, a Muslim must be free to serve Allah alone, no matter where he lives.

The Prophet (S) told Allah's commandment to Muslims. They all replied to him they would go wherever he would ask them to go, though all of them loved their city, Makkah, and their homes. But the Muslims loved their Prophet (S) and their religion more than their lives, their country, and their homes. They were prepared to do everything for the sake of Allah.

Rasulullah (S) asked them to go to Yathrib one by one so that the *Kuffar* would not notice it. Rasulullah (S), being their leader, stayed until all of them were safely gone. Finally, only Rasulullah(S), his close friend, Abu Bakr(R), his loving cousin, Ali(R) and a few other helpless Muslims were left. Makkans had seen how Muslims had quietly disappeared. They feared that if Prophet Muhammad(S) went to Yathrib, he would become very powerful. Yathrib was on the northern trade route of the Makkan caravan. Muslim power in Yathrib could become a threat to their business and trade. The best solution, they thought, was to kill the Prophet(S).

Rasulullah(S) used to go to Kabah very early in the morning for *Salat*. All the Makkans decided to unite to kill Prophet Muhammad (S) because they feared revenge from the family of Banu Hashim. All the leaders of the various tribes in Makkah decided to surround his house at night and to attack him together.

Allah, through a revelation, told Rasulullah(S) about the plans of the *Kuffar*. The night that the *Kuffar* surrounded his house, Rasulullah(S) was asked by Allah to leave for Yathrib. He had to pass through the *Kuffar* who were well armed and ready to kill him. This was a test for Muhammad's faith in divine commandment. Rasulullah (S) was obedient to Allah and had no fears of the consequences.

He had one big problem which he had to settle before leaving. He had a lot of things from the Makkans which he was keeping in trust. The Makkans did not believe in him as a prophet, but they had full faith in him as an honest person. There were no bank safes in those days. People wanted to entrust their things to someone whom they trusted. Since Rasulullah (S) was trusted by all the Makkans, both Muslims and non-Muslims brought their jewelry, money, and other valuables to Rasulullah(S) for safe custody. Thus, Rasulullah(S) had many such things in trust for others. He must return them before he could leave.

This way, he tried to show us that a Muslim must always be just, honest, and trustworthy, even to his enemies and even when he faces a threat to his life.

Rasulullah (S) asked Ali (R), his cousin, to stay and return these things to their owners the next morning. Ali(R), was very brave. He was so happy to be serving the Prophet(S) that he went to sleep in the bed of Rasulullah(S). People stood outside to kill the Prophet(S). But Ali(R) had no fears. He did not care about death if it came while serving Rasulullah(S). His faith was firm. Later he said,"I had the best sleep of my life that night."

Late at night, when Rasulullah (S) came out, he saw his house surrounded by the *Kuffar* He recited the verse from *Surah YaSin*, "And We (Allah) have covered them and they cannot see."(36:9). Allah made the *Kuffar's* eyes temporarily blind. They could not see Rasulullah(S) as he left.

He went to the house of his dear friend, Abu Bakr (R), and then together they left for Yathrib.

Points of review:

1. The *Kuffar* decided to kill Rasulullah(S) and one night surrounded his house.

2. Allah helped Rasulullah (S) to leave his house safely, and the *Kuffar* did not see him..

3. Ali (R) stayed behind to return the things of other people that Rasulullah (S) kept in trust.

Words to remember

Custody, entrust, *Hijrah*.

Quranic Study:

1. The Quran teaches us never to betray the trust and to return the deposits to their owners.

   Read, *al-Baqarah* 2:283 *al-Nisa* 4:58; *al-Anfal* 8:27; *al-Mu'minun* 23:8; *al-Ma'arij* 70:32

2. The Muslim society cannot be built on law and regulations alone but personal qualities of its members' character. Read *Surah Isra'* 17:22-39, 53, 78, 79.

   What qualities of character does Allah want the Muslims to possess?

LESSON 19

KUFFAR SEARCH FOR RASULULLAH (S)
First Year of Hijrah

Rasulullah(S) and Abu Bakr(R) knew that in the morning *Kuffar* would discover their flight. The *Kuffars'* search parties would try to chase them. So they went a short distance and hid in the cave called *Thawr* to avoid the search parties.

In the morning when the *Kuffar* did not see the Prophet (S) come out, they went inside. They found Ali (R) sleeping in the Prophet's bed. They were enraged. Ali(R) told them that Rasulullah(S) had left as they stood guard. The *Kuffar* were disappointed. They knew that the Prophet (S) would go to Yathrib, so they went towards Yathrib after him.

They announced a big prize for his capture. Many prize seekers went out to capture Rasulullah (S). They found no trace of him. In fact, some came up to the cave of Thawr. Some even thought to go inside to look for him. When Abu Bakr (R) heard this, he became worried for the safety of Rasulullah (S). But Rasulullah (S) consoled him, "What do you think of those two whose third one is Allah." Allah was indeed the third one with them. He sent *Sakinah* — peace of mind and calm — to them which removed all anxiety from their hearts. Besides, Allah also made a spider weave a web at the door of the cave and a dove lay eggs at the entrance. When the *Kuffar* looked at the entrance and saw the web and eggs they thought no one could go inside. Thus, Allah miraculously saved Rasulullah (S) and Abu Bakr (R) from their enemies.

For three days, both Rasulullah (S) and his friend, Abu Bakr (R), stayed in that narrow cave. Each evening Abu Bakr's daughter, Asma' (R) would send some milk and food through her servant. Abu Bakr's young son came at night quietly with the news of the enemies' plans. He told them the *Kuffar* had offered a big prize for the arrest or murder of Rasulullah (S). Many greedy people had gone out in every direction to look for him.

After three days stay in the cave, Rasulullah (S) and Abu Bakr (R) came out. Abu Bakr's servant had two camels ready for them. They set out for Yathrib. They continued traveling day and night. They wanted to get to Yathrib as soon as possible.

At noon it was too hot to go on, so they sat down to rest under the shadow of a big stone. A shepherd offered them some milk. For several days, the famous Arab rider, Suraqa, had been searching for them. He saw them resting. He was happy and thought he had already earned the big prize. But Prophet (S) was not afraid to see him. Then, all of a sudden, the heels of Suraqa's horse got stuck in the sand. Suraqa felt very very embarrassed. Now he realized that Allah was protecting His Prophet (S) and Abu Bakr (R). He went to Rasulullah (S) and gave himself up. Rasulullah (S) forgave him. Suraqa became a devoted Muslim.

In that helpless condition Rasulullah (S) addressed Suraqa, "What do you, O Suraqa, think of the day when you will wear the precious expensive bangles of Khusraw, the emperor of Iran, in your hand."

Little did Suraqa understand the prophecy of Rasulullah (S). Fourteen years later, the second *Khalifa*, Umar (R), offered these bangles to Suraqa as the power of Khusraw was shattered by Muslim armies.

The party of Rasulullah (S) made another stop at the tent of a lady called Ummi Ma'bad. She welcomed them and discovered they were hungry. She said, "I don't have anything to offer except the milk of my goat. But its milk is dried up due to lack of food."

Rasulullah (S) touched the udders of the goat and they milked it. The goat provided enough milk for the family and guests. As Rasulullah's party left, Ummi Ma'bad's husband came and heard the story of the blessed guests.

He said, "By God, these are the same people that the Quraish are searching for. I will become Muhammad's servant and follower."

After some rest, Rasulullah (S) and Abu Bakr (R) continued their journey. In Yathrib the news of Rasulullah's arrival had already reached the people. They were anxious to welcome the Prophet (S). Finally, Rasulullah (S) and Abu Bakr (R) arrived at Quba, a town three miles outside of Yathrib. They stayed there for a fortnight. Even in those few days, he built a *Masjid* there. This *Masjid* is still in Quba. Thousands of Pilgrims go there to say their special *Salat*.

Ali (R), who left Makkah later, joined Rasulullah (S) in Quba. Rasulullah (S) was pleased to see Ali (R) arrive safely. It was time to move on to their final destination, the city of Yathrib, which was eagerly awaiting the arrival of its honored guest.

In part II of the book we shall read how Rasulullah (S) was received in Madinah, what challenges did he face there and how did he succeed in establishing a united Muslim *Ummah* and an Islamic State?

Points of review:

1. Rasulullah(S) and Abu Bark(R) hid in the cave for three days.
2. They arrived safely at Quba.
3. Rasulullah(S) built a *Masjid* in Quba.

Words to remember:

Udders.

Important names

Abu Bakr(R) Quba, Suraqa, Ummi Ma'bad.

Quranic Study

1. Allah describes the incident of the cave in the Quran *(al-Tawbah* 9:40). Read and see how Allah helps the believers when they are in anxiety.

2. *Sakinah* — the peace and tranquility — is mentioned in the Quran in many places, e.g. *al-Fath* 48:4, 18, 26; *al-Tawabah* 9:26, 40. Read these verses to understand its meaning.

3. Read the verse *al-Tawabah* 9:108. What is the basis on which the *Masjid* of Quba is built? What kind of people built such *Masjid?*